SELL
YOUR
KNOWLEDGE

*The Professional's Guide to
Winning More Business*

MONICA NICOU
CHRISTINE RIBBING &
EVA ÅDING

KOGAN
PAGE

To our clients

First published in 1994

Kogan Page Limited
120 Pentonville Road
London N1 9JN

© Monica Nicou, Christine Ribbing and Eva Åding, 1994

British Library Cataloguing in Publication Data

A CIP record for this book is available from the British Library.

ISBN 0 7494 1366 2

Typeset by Saxon Graphics Ltd, Derby
Printed in England by Clays Ltd, St Ives plc

Contents

Foreword

This is a timely book for all professionals now faced with a new, demanding and challenging environment. It focuses on today's challenge to master the skills and knowledge necessary to create and manage competitive relationships in an increasingly knowledge-intensive business world.

The so called third wave is sweeping through the world, bringing great changes to society and especially industry and commerce. We are all aware that the industrial sector is no longer reporting growth, but that the growth potential is found in the service sector, which in turn is becoming ever more knowledge-intensive. The knowledge-intensive professional firms will inevitably increase their share of the market, locally as well as globally. The drive is towards specialization and knowledge-intensive market-oriented services.

We are well aware that our business is all about people and clients— our two markets. The focus of this book on *knowledge* as the power for business development and the most valuable magnet to attract both clients and people, draws attention to a new dimension not only for leaders of knowledge-intensive professional organizations, but also for all other professionals in their daily work.

For natural reasons, all professionals have a tendency to prioritize technical ability over client needs, and issues such as leadership in knowledge-intensive organizations have remained in the background. Professionals often act as if knowledge and marketing were contradictory by nature. Now the challenge is to create an environment and culture that incites the winning combination of technical excellence and market adaption, knowing that specialists are not always sufficiently market oriented.

This book gives not only an interesting structure of theory, but also valuable practical suggestions.

Although one might say that services are delivered locally, professional organizations will find that their markets are becoming increasingly global as their customers move across borders to new markets. Global services require global competence and constant awareness of the state of the art.

During my years as President of IFAC (International Federation of Accountants), representing more than one million professional accountants in practice, industry and public service all over the globe, I recognized the growth of the profession, in the new markets, as well as the aspects referred to in this book. Many professionals around the world will certainly find this book well worth reading.

Bertil Edlund
Chairman of Coopers & Lybrand, Sweden and
member of the Board of Coopers & Lybrand International

About the authors

Monica Nicou and *Eva Åding* are senior consultants, working as trainers and advisers to leaders and professionals. They are partners in Pro Competence Associates, a consultancy specializing in business and competence development in knowledge-intensive organizations.

Christine Ribbing trains professionals how to present their concepts to international audiences. Her firm, Christine Ribbing Language and Communication, focuses on generative learning skills, including the business applications of Neuro-linguistic Programming, NLP.

Acknowledgements

Our sincere gratitude to all those leaders and professionals mentioned in this book who have given us their time to provide us with examples from their own organizations.

We would also like to thank our colleagues, friends and families for valuable dialogues that have contributed to the formation of our thinking. In particular, we would like to mention our colleague B M Ahrnell with whom we established the first building blocks of 'knowledge marketing'.

Introduction

'We have moved from knowledge to knowledges'
Peter Drucker

THE NEW CURRENCY

The business world of the 1990s is on the brink of a new economy in which the raw materials are information and knowledge. The focus of business leaders, economists, politicians and investors is shifting increasingly from 'hard', tangible assets such as iron and steel to 'soft', intangible assets like people's creativity and knowledge. These assets are mainly individual and those who possess them are known as 'knowledge workers' or 'knowledge professionals'. They process knowledge for the benefit of both customers/clients and their own organizations — knowledge organizations.

In this book we address everyone who considers themselves knowledge professionals and every organization that identifies itself as being knowledge based. As a result we believe this book will be of interest to all professionals and organizations which need to make the most of their ability to identify and communicate the value of their knowledge. We have anchored our book on the conviction that, apart from being the most valuable asset in an organization, knowledge is also the most valuable magnet to attract both clients and employees. As Thomas Stewart points out in his *Fortune* article 'Brain-power, How Intellectual Capital is Becoming America's Most Valuable Asset', 'it's the sum of everything everybody in your company knows that gives you a competitive edge in the marketplace.' Knowledge organizations are built on relationships with both clients and employees. The basis for creating and retaining these relationships is the knowledge contained within the organization.

THE VALUE-ADDING CHAIN OF BUSINESS

In *Sell Your Knowledge* we deal specifically with business development and marketing in business-to-business markets. In contrast to a handicraft, which is designed and produced by one person, a modern, complex product or service is the result of hundreds or thousands of different people's coordinated knowledge and activities. The process of producing a new medicine, for example, involves the work of a whole range of in-house experts as well as external consultants and suppliers.

The chain of the activities which add value to products and services can be referred to as the value-adding chain of business (illustrated in Figure 1). There are many links in this chain, eg research and development, purchasing, production, marketing and sales, supply and service, support, corporate communication and investor relations. To strengthen each link, several kinds of knowledge have to be added from experts in different fields, such as technology, environment, quality, venture capital, negotiation, finance, healthcare, risk management, auditing and advertising, as well as the more general knowledge of management, leadership and training. The main threads running through all these kinds of knowledge are information technology and communication skills.

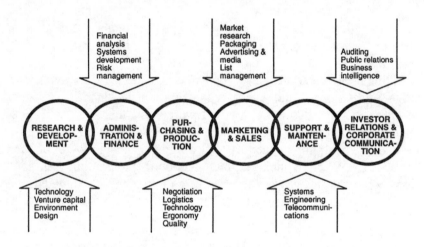

Figure 1   The value-adding chain of business

FROM KNOWLEDGE TO KNOWLEDGES

In *Post-Capitalist Society*, Peter Drucker says: 'We have moved from knowledge to knowledges'. Drucker identifies knowledge as having previously been the preserve of educated people whose use of knowledge was primarily intrinsic. As life in Western economies has become externally oriented to a very high degree, knowledge is now tested in action. This kind of knowledge is focused on results which are found outside the individual — in society, the economy, or in the advancement of knowledge itself. As a result, the different streams of knowledge are becoming increasingly manifold and specialized. They are inter- and intraorganizational, produced both internally (by internal staff units, eg training, computer, marketing and information departments) and externally (by consultants and other suppliers).

Since business is dependent on results, knowledge professionals have to constantly develop new ideas, learn and apply new kinds of knowledge and toss out any dead wood that no longer bears fruit. *Sell Your Knowledge* challenges knowledge professionals to:

■ leverage knowledge—ie create client value with it;
■ produce new knowledge;
■ make others know that they know how to do this.

In the increasingly complex business world, knowledge as competitive strategy goes beyond products and services. The more complicated products and services become, the more buyers and clients will have to cling to the intangible aspects of their buying decision, their confidence in the vendor's knowledge and reliability.

From our everyday experience as business consultants, we have learnt that success follows those companies and professionals who develop expertise and know how to communicate it through demonstrating that it benefits their markets and clients.

Discovering the power of your knowledge as a competitive edge can in fact prove to be a major turning point! Among our client companies we often hear reflections like: 'Before we used to focus our market communication on describing our own success, qualifications and outstanding service performance. Through turning our minds 180 degrees we discovered the hidden asset of our knowledge. We have learned how to creatively use our knowledge to focus on our clients' situation, problems and opportunities.' or 'We suddenly saw that our expertise was *the* magnet that through better use would attract both the right clients and the best prospective employees. We saw that learning and communicating our knowledge had to be our prime strategy.'

Very little research has been carried out into managing client relationships. In this book we mainly base our theories, concepts and ideas on the practical results our clients have achieved and on our reflections from interviews with leaders and professionals in successful knowledge organizations. We have also drawn conclusions from our own marketing experiences as consultants, and the examples our colleagues from around the world have contributed.

Sell Your Knowledge is not only for partners, managers and leaders in knowledge-based organizations. To develop successful client relationships, all professionals have to be proactively involved in strategy and practice. Therefore this book is for all professionals in the knowledge-based organization.

It is not our intention to present the 'gospel truth' or a finished concept—adept business people have always worked along the lines we recommend. Rather, our approach is to provide a structure for selective business planning in knowledge-based organizations. The book is also intended as a source of inspiration and a means for professionals to share their values concerning business, marketing, client relationships, market communication, quality, learning and in-house communication.

References

Drucker, Peter F (1993) *Post-Capitalist Society*, Butterworth-Heinemann, Oxford.

Stewart, Thomas A (1991) 'Brain power, how intellectual capital is becoming America's most valuable asset', *Fortune*, June 3.

1

Multiprofessional Markets

'All economic organization is fast becoming
"knowledge plays".'

Tom Peters

This chapter outlines the different kinds of knowledge organizations
and the environment in which they work.

Professionals who offer their clients expertise and knowledge
cannot delegate their business development to marketing or sales
departments. This is because their source of business development
lies in the transfer of knowledge between themselves and their clients.
Traditional industrial companies can divide their functions into
departments for design/quality, purchasing, production, marketing,
sales, etc. In the knowledge company, however, *all* professionals have
to develop their 'product' (knowledge), create client relationships
(market), develop understanding of these clients' needs and suggest
solutions/knowledges/products (sell). They also have to cooperate
with clients, creating both service quality and results (produce).

This is the multifunctional role of the knowledge professional,
focusing on proactive behaviour. The marketing of a professional firm
or other knowledge-based organization is the sum of all the activities
and behaviour of all the professionals in that firm in relation to
markets and clients, other external contacts and in-house colleagues.
Despite this fact, few academic programmes have this type of marketing on their syllabuses. Specific marketing skills for knowledge
professionals have unfortunately been left to trial and error.

WHY KNOWLEDGE NEEDS TO BE MARKETED

Professional service firms face more critical buyers

Professional service firms worldwide are facing a new competitive situation. Professionals such as lawyers, accountants, architects, engineers and surveyors are having to develop marketing skills in order to survive. As a result, clients are able to take advantage of a wide choice of options from which they can buy the knowledge they need at a favourable price.

Furthermore, information technology will rapidly 'enhance the base level' in many professional fields, in ways which have not yet been experienced. A whole professional practice is able to be reinvented if the world's leading experts make their knowledge and experience available through information databases and expert systems. For example, the efficiency and productivity of law firms has been enhanced through a database called Pacta, created in Sophia Antipolis, France. This continually updated database is 'packaged knowledge', an electronic library which integrates the accumulated knowledge of 155 leading international lawyers. Pacta covers the most common documents and advice a business will need throughout its life-cycle, including incorporation documents, agreements for partners and shareholders, employment agencies and distributors, leasing and licensee agreements, advice on commercial disputes and tax.

Pacta will enhance the standards and efficiency of a professional field which has traditions dating back to the fifteenth century. Previously you could reinvent the wheel for every client and make them pay for it. Now, however, databases and expert systems will have a dramatic effect on the client's expectations concerning value for money.

Less traditional professional service markets, such as financial advisers and insurance brokers, computer and software consultants, also face more critical buyers. As Beth Summers says, 'Many companies have just begun to realize that information service providers are among their highest non-payroll budget items. They are beginning to apply this enhanced cost awareness to other vendors (eg consultants, lawyers and accountants).'

Undiscovered opportunities for knowledge-based industries

Peter Winiger, senior consultant in marketing, market research and new products/services development at ATAG, Ernst & Young

Consulting (Basel, Switzerland), has extensive experience in developing high-tech companies. He maintains that high-tech companies can gain from viewing themselves as knowledge companies: 'In spite of the fact that they sell products, more than 50 per cent of the price paid by the customer is related to application-connected tests, advice, pilot-runs on the manufacturer's own test-rigs, feasibility studies, engineering and technical support as well as know-how transfer from industry to industry.'

Many high-tech companies are currently trying to answer the questions: How can we make better use of the knowledge we have stored for decades? How can we leverage the knowledge we have obtained through our collaboration with our market, through our research and development of products and through our own internal development programmes? How can we turn these hidden assets into business?

The identified needs of today's business community have already been exceeded by the technology currently available. So now the knowledge element of technology has become the mainstay of business cost efficiency. As a result, many companies that produce high-tech products are in the process of transforming themselves into professional service firms. They are positioning themselves as co-producers of their clients' corporate strategies and exploring how their products can act as a vehicle for marketing not only services but also knowledge, for example in terms of training and consultancy services.

How can high-tech industries gain from developing the knowledge part of their offering? Possible approaches are for them to:

- create new business by selling their knowledge in the form of consultancy, education and/or development programmes;
- generate income for marketing through selling knowledge;
- change their image through being connected with sharing knowledge instead of relying on traditional sales slogans (buyers want suppliers with credibility);
- strengthen their relationship with their customers through becoming partners in the latter's development instead of simply being suppliers;
- reorganize their marketing and sales function, making the specialists the creators and developers not only of products but also of client relationships. Customers do not want to speak to salespeople—they want to talk to the experts.

Internal services and staff units are put under pressure

With ongoing decentralization, more 'power' and responsibility are being given to individual operating divisions. As a result, staff units are put under pressure. Human resource development, training, computer services, information, quality, purchase and marketing functions are internal functions that have to face a new reality. Various departments are currently being reorganized as internal profit centres or service companies within a corporation. The former authoritarian staff members are expected to act in a new role, as internal consultants or service providers, identifying and serving clients in competition with external suppliers. Some also have to cover their costs or develop their knowledge by selling some 10–20 per cent of their time to external markets.

Learning how to operate in a competitive situation is frustrating for many professionals and has created a demand for training in business development, marketing and customer relationships. Conferences for internal experts take up issues such as 'Marketing the training function' or 'How to work as an internal IT consultant'.

The new 'business-within-the-business' has to be able to create a demand for its knowledge and services, to contribute and communicate in a way that gives it a reputation for being a strategic asset—not a cost centre. To get to grips with the new situation, the staff unit has to develop a vision and a business plan. Today's staff unit must have a leader engaging his or her people in the process of:

- identifying clients and their needs for knowledge and services;
- identifying the value embodied in the unit's 'business idea';
- communicating that value to create a demand and developing mutually beneficial client relationships;
- identifying and investing in the new knowledge needed to make the corporation competitive in tomorrow's marketplace.

This process is the process of knowledge marketing.

Marketing to communicate the need for change

Non-profit organizations also create value-adding services—the values that transform people to transform society. But how can the contribution of these organizations be made most effective? Peter Drucker says that 'The Girl Scouts, the Red Cross, the pastoral churches—our nonprofit organizations—are becoming America's management leaders. In two areas, strategy and the effectiveness of the board, they are practising what most American businesses only preach. And in the most crucial area—the motivation and the productivity of knowledge workers—they are truly pioneers, working out the policies and practices that business will have to learn tomorrow.'

Movements and associations can also be leaders in marketing if they understand the impact of education as a means of transforming values.

Authorities and other public knowledge-intensive services

The growing tendency to deregulate and orient authorities towards the market, sometimes even to privatize them, creates a huge need for marketing ability among publicly employed professionals in, for example, treasury departments, employment agencies and medical centres. For these professionals, marketing services is not enough. As they market knowledge and skills, they can benefit from knowing more about how to market their knowledge.

CROSS-DISCIPLINARY MARKETING

The search for new knowledge and new combinations of knowledge has contributed to today's international business environment of decentralization, networking and joint venturing. In fact, the more knowledge intensive a business is, the more difficult it is to apply traditional business concepts. 'Ever heard of the virtual corporation?' This question is put to readers in a cover story in *Business Week*.

'The virtual corporation is a temporary network of independent companies—suppliers, customers, even erstwhile rivals—linked by information technology to share skills, costs and access to one another's markets. It will have neither central office nor organization chart. It will have not hierarchy, not vertical integration.' The concept fits well in the context of the value-adding chain. It captures the image of an organization based on alliances and joint ventures, in contrast to traditional organizations, where ownership, hierarchy and control are the keys. The parties in a virtual corporation concentrate on and develop their core competences and buy all other knowledge and services from external providers.

In an era of specialization, the need to market one's knowledge increases. More and more people are working in cross-disciplinary teamwork and projects, eg when marketing and production people are involved with scientists at early stages in the product development process. This means that one kind of knowledge has to be 'sold' to people possessing other knowledge, internally or externally, enabling potential team members and business partners to understand the expertise offered. Furthermore, knowledge-based markets, intra- as well as interorganizational, are as invisible as the 'merchandise' that is transferred. The existence of multiprofessional markets means that professionals have to be able both to identify needs for their knowledge and to communicate it to clients to whom it will be of benefit.

The need for cross-disciplinary 'marketing' has been highlighted by Drucker in *Post-Capitalist Society*: 'We neither need nor will get "polymaths" who are at home in many knowledges. We will probably become even more specialized. But what we do need—and what will define the Educated Person in the Knowledge Society—is ability to *understand* the knowledges. What is each about? What are its central theories? What major new insights has it produced?'

To facilitate this process, professionals have to market their knowledge, their insights and ideas, make them concrete and perceivable by applying them to the problems of the surrounding world. It is the responsibility of each field of expertise to market its knowledge to other fields, thus creating visible markets. If they fail to do this, their knowledge will remain invisible and worthless.

The term 'knowledge professionals' refers to professionals in different fields of knowledge, eg pharmacists, financial advisers, psychologists. We view the professional service firm as a role model for other organizations. As Tom Peters points out: 'All firms are becoming professional service firms.'

This is true not only in terms of organization but also in terms of business development, client relationship management, marketing and competence development—all areas which we cover in this book. Knowledge company/organization therefore refers to professional service firms, high-tech companies, internal staff units, movements, associations, knowledge-intensive authorities and others that want to identify themselves with this concept. The nature of business-to-business knowledge has the following implication for marketing: talking about client relationships and personal relationships rather than customer relationships and public relations.

'HIGH-TECH/HIGH-TOUCH' MARKETPLACES

'Language and technology, an interrelated pair, gave man a lever.'
                                                                E T Hall

This quotation catches the essence of the knowledge-based business world. High-tech dialogues characterize knowledge marketplaces where information and communication technology is the vital nerve. High-touch refers to closeness in client relationships and personal interaction between professionals and clients. Electronic communication 'highways' pave the way for new patterns of infrastructure to enable information and artificial intelligence to be transmitted between computer networks in real time.

To complement technology, trading in knowledge requires trust and relationships to be established. These are created through dialogues and meetings in which individuals can establish a process to share their knowledge, ideas and values. Wherever there is knowledge to be offered, there are people. Knowledge markets thrive in interactive and educational environments such as conferences and seminars. As Alan Webber states in a *Harvard Business Review* article, 'the most important work in the new economy is creating conversations . . . One of the many paradoxes of the new economy is that conversation—traditionally regarded as a waste of time—is in fact the key resource for competing on time.'

CLIENT RELATIONSHIPS ARE EVERYONE'S RESPONSIBILITY

As a knowledge professional, your marketing wealth lies in your competence and behaviour. The marketing concepts described in this book are a combination of administrative and behavioural aspects. Strategic thinking, goal orientation, proactive behaviour and knowledge about marketing tools are essential for managers and team members in knowledge-intensive organizations.

The following chapters guide you through a series of steps to familiarize you with business development, marketing and professional development from an 'outside-in' perspective. You learn how to see the client's point of view and to think in terms of benefits for your clients, rather than giving detailed accounts of your company's qualifications and methods. All this puts a high premium on your relationships with your clients.

We emphasize that to create business from knowledge you need to:

- identify the value and results which your knowledge creates for both clients and your own organization;
- develop and retain long-term client relationships;
- involve every professional in proactive behaviour to create goals and markets.

In the knowledge company this process is integrated into daily business and collaboration with clients.

THE VALUE OF YOUR KNOWLEDGE

To highlight the importance of evaluating and communicating your individual knowledge and that of your organization, let us look to the world of art and one of the greatest artistic geniuses of the twentieth century, Pablo Picasso. One day, in a café, Picasso was approached by an American woman. She begged him to make a quick sketch for her on the back of a paper napkin. Picasso duly obliged, gave the lady her sketch and said it would cost $5000. The woman was aghast and asked him how the sketch could possibly cost so much when it had only taken three minutes to produce. 'Madame', said Picasso, 'it didn't take three minutes, it took 30 years.'

To market your knowledge, you need an awareness of your own knowledge and the ability to create value from it. Since many professionals and professional organizations are not fully aware themselves of their true competences, they are unable to create an awareness of their knowledge in others. As a result, such professionals and organizations are not in a position to set in motion the type of activities which would make other people more aware.

It is not your knowledge that counts: it is what you do with it! The fact that knowledge is a resource controlled by the professionals who possess it has created a shift of power. In *Managing Knowhow*, Sveiby and Lloyd maintain, 'The shift of power away from those who have and towards those who do challenges many of the presumptions and prejudices embedded in company law.'

The nature of knowledge has also changed the nature of responsibility—the responsibility for what one does with one's knowledge. It is every knowledge professional's responsibility to ask the critical question, 'Do I use my knowledge and capability optimally to create maximum value for society, my organization, myself?' Knowing more about how to market your knowledge gives you the power to use that knowledge in the way that *you* think is best.

References

Bryan, John A, Richard Brandt and Otis Port (1993), 'The Virtual Corporation', *Business Week*, February 8.

Drucker, Peter F (1993) *Post-Capitalist Society*, Butterworth-Heinemann, Oxford.

Hall, Edward T (1973) *The Silent Language*, Anchor Press/Doubleday, New York.

Peters, Tom (1992) *Liberation Management: Necessary Disorganization for the Nanosecond Nineties*, Alfred A Knopf, New York.

Summers, Beth (1992) 'Smart Q & A', *Services Marketing Today*, Vol 8, No 6, November/December, American Marketing Association, Chicago.

Sveiby, Karl Erik and Tom Lloyd (1987) *Managing Knowhow*, Bloomsbury, London.

Webber, Alan M (1993) 'What's So New about the New Economy?', *Harvard Business Review,* January–February.

2

Create Business from Knowledge

*'Professionals get paid for their time but that's not what we
sell. We sell knowledge and skill.'*
David H Maister

This chapter highlights the characteristics of knowledge as merchandise and a competitive tool. It also introduces the marketing framework used by knowledge companies.

REASSESS YOUR BUSINESS AND MARKETING CONCEPTS

Whatever knowledge-intensive business you are in, you may sometimes ask yourself: How can we create and retain the business relationships we want? Which areas of our marketing are unexplored and how can we define unique selling points? How should we position ourselves in the minds of our preferred clients? The quest for new keys to business development and marketing continues. In the 1980s the key was service. In the 1990s, the key word is knowledge.

Is knowledge your business? Consider the accumulated knowledge of your organization and ask yourself the crucial question: Do we use all this knowledge to produce services for our clients, or do we offer our knowledge to increase the value we create for our clients? If knowledge is your 'product' you will recognize your business idea in the following statement: The aim we have for our clients is to enhance their competitiveness through:

■ development;

- improvement;
- problem solving.

This is achieved through the transfer of knowledge between you and your client. If knowledge is your business you do not market ready-made, packaged services. On the contrary, you use your knowledge and experience to help your clients to identify and define unique problems and needs and then suggest solutions. You work in close interaction with your clients, involving them, cooperating with them. You work in projects rather than running operations, applying and adapting your knowledge to the different clients' special problems and needs. The result of your work may not show until much later; it may take months or years before you and your client have implemented your advice and can measure the results. Buying your knowledge must be considered by the client as an investment rather than a cost.

THE DIFFERENCES THAT MATTER IN MARKETING

Knowledge-intensive organizations offer a wide spectrum of intangible commodities. We need to look into those intangibles in more detail and discuss what we are going to market and how. To simplify, let us begin by dividing the intangibles into two categories—services and knowledge—in order to develop our awareness about the differences between them and the implications of those differences for our business development and marketing.

Services save time and effort

The word 'service' comes from the Latin *servus*, 'slave', and means work done for others as an occupation or business. In our context it means to carry out tasks for customers. Services are often packaged (pre-defined, named and priced), and as such they are often described by the seller as 'products'. Services aim at creating convenience and saving time and effort for the customer. The service provider takes over responsibility for the activity.

'Facilities management' is one example of a service. The customer 'outsources' its information processing in order to be released from the problems of managing and maintaining the information system. This saves time and energy and the customer pays for not having to be involved, leaving the responsibility to the service provider. The customer does not have to spend time thinking about the quality of the service as long as an acceptable level is maintained.

Knowledge creates change

The transfer of knowledge, eg advice, education or coaching, aims to initiate the improvement and development of the clients. What they buy is not convenience but a result in terms of enhanced competitiveness for their businesses.

The process towards this development is often experienced as the opposite of convenience—it is quite demanding for the client. Knowledge providers do not take over problems, since clients are the ones who 'own' their problems. The role of the knowledge provider is to initiate and facilitate change by acting as an investigator, analyst, creator, innovator, adviser, teacher, coach, initiator, inspirer, motivator, catalyst, and so on.

The creation and implementation of a computer software system can be used as an example of knowledge, which is adapted specifically to a company's needs to develop its business. It aims at initiating the development of this business and improving its competitiveness. The knowledge of the consultant is focused on helping to identify the problems and opportunities of the client company, defining the needs and suggesting solutions to the problems, transferring knowledge to the users of the system.

A systems consultant we worked with explained: 'Our role is to leave an ability behind us.' An auditor put it this way: 'Each year we see to it that our client takes a step forward.' This we call creating added value.

Consultants help their clients to develop new opportunities or to avoid threats. As such they have to involve and cooperate with them, constantly striving to enhance the abilities of the client organizations. Providing knowledge means contributing to growth and this cannot be done without the clients taking an active part. It should be stressed again that it is the client who owns the problem and who therefore has the ultimate responsibility for solving it.

When you analyse what you offer your market, consider the spectrum from services to knowledge and identify where your own offerings are (see Figure 2.1).

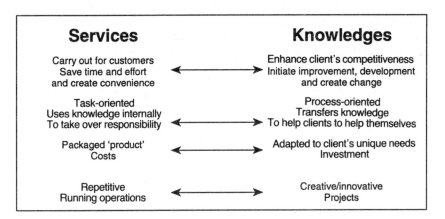

Figure 2.1 The services–knowledge spectrum

Your knowledge attracts

It has to be pointed out that a huge array of knowledge is needed to create, manage and supply both services *and* knowledge. The main difference has to do with how your company uses its knowledge. Do you produce services *for* customers using your knowledge internally? Or do you transfer knowledge to your clients in order to facilitate the development of their competitiveness?

A consultancy firm, for example, can deliver reports (services), but most also become involved in the implementation phase, through giving advice and providing development programmes and seminars for management and staff (knowledge). A research centre can carry out research (services), but many also spread their results to society and the business world by means of presentations, seminars, reports and articles (knowledge). Accountancy firms offer both services and knowledge. The audit/review is a service and makes up the largest part of the auditing firm's turnover. Advisory services, eg taxation or financial advice, constitute value-adding knowledge that demands a great deal of interchange and transfer of knowledge between the accountants/consultants and the clients.

Many professional businesses obtain most of their revenue from services. But what makes their clients choose a particular business rather than one of its competitors? Most probably it is the knowledge and the expected quality and results of the advice which that business will provide. Stockbrokers or merchant bankers, for example, offer both services in the form of trading and knowledge in the form of investment and financial advice. There is no doubt that it is their knowledge that is the competitive tool. Their clients identify them as a knowledge company rather than as a service business.

LEVERAGING SERVICES TO CREATE KNOWLEDGE

Services can be the source of the information which will create business from knowledge.

Marine Advisory Services represents one of the major business areas within **SSPA Maritime Consulting**. It assists shipbuilders, designers of high-speed craft as well as merchant ships, with knowledge and services within the area of ship hydrodynamics. SSPA Maritime Consulting's core competence and business have developed from model testing (service) in its own maritime dynamics laboratory, which consists of ocean basins and towing tanks. With information compiled from these tests, the hydrodynamics experts create an information database. From this they develop calculation tools, software and readily available basic designs, which enable them to offer shipbuilders advice on design and hull optimization and predictions about sea-keeping and manoeuvring (knowledge).

Marine Advisory Services has made a synthesis of its services and knowledge, accumulating knowledge from its service business, thus developing its knowledge business. This is often done in such fields as healthcare, insurance and HRD, among others.

Transforming the internal service unit

A growing number of internal service providers are currently reevaluating their roles, transforming their practices from service units into internal competence/knowledge centres. To develop towards a knowledge provider means leaving the old role as a service producer, carrying out certain tasks for internal clients. It means developing an understanding of which competences are crucial to attaining the organization's business goals, developing those core competences and striving to transfer them internally, thus helping internal clients (line managers) to enhance their performance with new knowledge. Many HRD departments are presently transforming themselves from administrators into a combination of controller, internal consultant and leader, identifying needs, marketing ideas and knowledge.

REDEFINING THE INDUSTRIAL COMPANY

Are you working in an industrial company? Consider the knowledge that you and your company have built up in the past few years:

- How have you used this knowledge to create optimal value for your market, your customers, your team and your organization?
- To what extent have you/your unit/team used your knowledge as a competitive tool in your marketing communication? Have you spread useful knowledge instead of simply promoting yourselves?
- How well have you used the opportunity to have your marketing financed by your clients? (Educative marketing can, in fact, be a source of profit and a business unit of its own. This kind of marketing includes educational programmes, seminars and conferences, databases, electronic books and other publications.)

Knowledge is an asset that you can give away—and yet keep. This gives you tremendous marketing opportunities. Knowledge is your raw material for marketing activities and creating your image. One industrial company which has redefined its business concepts in order to maximize the link between products, services and knowledge is described below.

Akzo Nobel Surface Chemistry provides specialty chemicals for a number of applications. Its business is knowledge intensive, with special emphasis on the environment. It has concluded that its customers' view of the company's knowledge is the most crucial success factor.

The management of Surface Chemistry have redefined their vision from an industrial company towards a knowledge-creating company, focusing on knowledge and relationships as its most important assets. They have defined their goals as to:

- focus on the development of knowledge;
- focus on the choice of long-term client/customer relationships;
- provide knowledge as well as services and products;
- try to understand unexpressed needs;
- work proactively as developers rather than sellers;
- involve and place demands on clients;
- adapt rapidly to change.

Akzo Nobel Surface Chemistry considers its vision as a strategic choice for the future, aiming at a higher degree of specialization and cost effectiveness. It will strive towards long-term relationships with its customers in order to jointly fulfil the latter's needs. It will aspire to choose customers, rather than let itself be chosen. It will involve those customers, seeking cooperation at higher levels in those organizations, initiating R&D and scientific councils.

This strategy has a great potential impact on the behaviour of employees. Learning within the company is focused, which means that everyone has the responsibility to teach and learn. All employees are responsible for taking part in creating and developing customer relationships, both externally and internally. Responsiveness, sensitivity and flexibility are encouraged.

Development to enable a company to make best use of its knowledge is sometimes enforced by its customers. 'Shockwaves keep coming' is the headline of a *Financial Times* survey of world automotive suppliers. Kevin Done, motor industry correspondent, concludes that 'The vehicle manufacturers are seeking to spread more of the research and development burden for new products on to the component makers. The leading suppliers are taking on the role of being systems producers, rather than suppliers.' This movement is referred to as 'relational manufacturing strategies' and puts the suppliers in a new marketing situation. In order to stay in the game when, for example, a Volkswagen division reduces the number of its suppliers from 1500 to 100–200 'logistical partners', a crucial ability for those partners will be to market concepts and knowledge about safety, comfort, security and mobile communications, instead of just a capacity to produce.

THE CHALLENGES OF KNOWLEDGE MARKETING

There is no demand

The marketing of services and simple products is based on the assumption that there is a demand. Such marketing rests on the belief that it is a matter of making the customer attracted to your specific offer, of an insurance package, for example, or a credit card service.

Most consultants or professionals, on the other hand, have no packaged services or products. Instead, they have the knowledge to solve unique problems and contribute to change.

They may also have specific methods, concepts or techniques for problem solving, but there is no point in describing them to a market that does not understand its own needs. Consultants' marketing is more a matter of identifying the unexpressed needs of their markets and marketing the problem, helping the chosen client categories to identify their own needs for development. It is the problems and needs that will have to be illuminated—not just the knowledge/service or product itself.

Expert systems development can be used as an example. Most organizations that could benefit from developing an internal expert system still have only a vague idea of what is involved. They are unaware of the opportunities that such a system might bring to the development of their business and competitiveness. Marketing such knowledge has to be a process of creating and selling ideas, pointing out needs and possibilities, in articles and presentations.

Put options, shareware, gestalt therapy, speed management, benchmarking, NLP, TQM—all these are kinds of knowledge and methods that have little or no market unless those who have the knowledge can create a consciousness of the need for them. Knowledge companies are ahead of their markets concerning the identification of the problems they can solve and possible results they can create. The challenge is to make markets understand their problems and needs and to create a confidence in the knowledge company's ability to help. *Tacit* knowledge is useless. A similar situation applies in immature product markets, eg alternative medicine or high-tech products.

Knowledge—'a pig in a poke'

The more complex or new the technique, method or product is, the more clients are inclined to make their choice of business partner on the basis of trust in the person. Selling a 'pig in a poke'—something bought unseen—means that you have to give time to the process of creating confidence in yourself, your knowledge and ability to help clients solve their problems.

The time perspectives of marketing and selling relate to the maturity of your relationship with clients and to the complexity or novelty of the knowledge or product that you want to sell. On the basis of asking several knowledge professionals about their time perspectives for different products and clients, we obtained the information summarized in Figure 2.2.

Selling old or known concepts/methods/techniques to an old/mature/long-standing client/customer, can be done in half an hour. However, to sell a new method/technique to a new client can take between one and three years. Consider the four fields in Figure 2.2. What time perspectives do you consider and work with in your marketing and business plans?

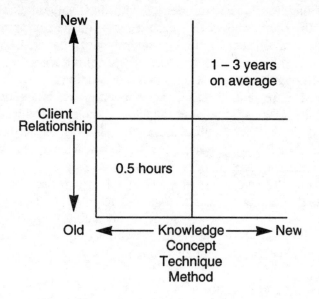

Figure 2.2 Time perspectives of knowledge marketing

Long-term commitments

With the growing complexity of products and techniques, the purchasing cycles of industrial markets tend to be increasingly stretched. Theodore Levitt has addressed relationship management in his classic *Harvard Business Review* article 'After the sale is over'. He describes the purchase cycles of some knowledge-intensive business fields, ranging from five to thirty years. According to Levitt, oil field installations have purchase cycles of 15–20 years, chemical plants 10–15 years, major components of a steel plant 20–30 years and a paper supply contract 5 years.

One of the observations made by Levitt is that buyer and seller become involved in a long-term relationship resembling that of a marriage. He says, 'Products are too complicated, repeat negotiations too much of a hassle and too costly. Under these conditions marketing is transformed into the inescapability of a relationship. Interface becomes interdependence.'

Knowledge needs relationships

The life-cycle of a product is usually described by a normal distribution curve, mirroring the launch, growth, maturity and decline of the product on its market. This implies that a product will sooner or later no longer be in demand and be replaced by other products. Knowledge providers, on the other hand, do not focus on a 'product'. They focus on something that has an eternal aspect—the business relationship—and so their goal is to create, develop and retain mutually beneficial relationships.

The emerging marketing concept of the 1990s is 'relationship marketing'. Martin Christopher, Adrian Payne and David Ballantyne have reviewed the focus and direction of marketing from 1950 to 1990. One important observation they make is that the nature of inter-relationships with customers is changing: 'The emphasis is moving from a transaction focus to a relationship focus.'

Traditional, transaction-based marketing, say these authors, focuses on single sales, is oriented towards product features, takes a short-term perspective, implies little customer commitment and limited customer contacts. In contrast, relationship marketing is focused on customer retention, is oriented towards client benefits and quality, takes a long-term perspective and implies a high degree of customer commitment.

Christopher, Payne and Ballantyne also question the usefulness of the 'Four Ps' model (Product, Price, Promotion and Place) which is the framework for traditional marketing: 'As such the basic "Four Ps" model does not really capture the full extent and complexity of marketing in practice, neither does it explicitly recognize the essential inter-relationships between the elements of the mix.'

Clients want experts

Client relationships cannot be delegated to a traditional sales force. Only knowledge-owners themselves have the knowledge and insights that give them the potential to develop and understand their clients' needs, to transform those needs into ideas for change and development and to communicate these ideas to potential markets and clients. The knowledge of each client's specific situation is as important as expertise. A client buys a person and wants continuity in the relationship.

The above points are mirrored in the following quotation from the 1992 annual report of the computer company Logica, 'It is clear that long-term relationships usually start from small beginnings, sometimes from the efforts of one key person who makes the difference which is recognized. Partnerships grow between people as much as between companies.'

Knowledge is not a 'consumer good'

The same knowledge will not be bought over and over again. Knowledge is not a 'consumer good' that will always be in demand. On the contrary, the challenge for a knowledge business partner is to develop knowledge in line with the clients' changing needs, so as to be able continuously to support their development and businesses. If efficiency and productivity are the keys of service management, learning and competence development are the key strategic factors of the knowledge company.

THE MODEL OF RELATIONSHIP MANAGEMENT

Relationship marketing puts a focus on creating and developing long-term, mutually beneficial client relationships on the basis of expertise and knowledge of the clients' needs. For the knowledge organization, relationship marketing has implications for every person interacting with the clients.

It increases the demand for insights into other people's behaviour, knowing how to act and behave in interaction with potential, present and former clients. The competence of a professional has to have a 'hard' and a 'soft' side.

Understanding and discussing the client relationship is vital to all people engaged in knowledge marketing. In this chapter we analyse the basic components of the client relationship with a view to enhancing knowledge professionals' ability to manage it and create optimal value. In future chapters, this model will be the structure for discussing marketing and quality development.

Client relationships can be divided into four phases (see Figure 2.3):

1. Arousing interest to attract clients.
2. Dialogue about the client's needs.
3. Collaboration in the assignment.
4. Follow-up, feedback and client care.

**The four phases
of the client relationship:**

4. Follow-up/
   Feedback

1. Arousing
   interest to
   attract clients

3. Collaboration

2. Dialogue about
   client's needs

Committed clients will recommend
you and act as ambassadors!

Figure 2.3 The four-phase model for relationship management

Phase 1: Arousing interest in your chosen markets to attract target clients

The first phase aims to attract and initiate contact with target clients in your chosen markets. Traditionally, marketing concentrates on this phase, as opposed to 'selling', which corresponds to the next phase.

A contact between two parties is the result of finding mutual interests. In the first phase the professionals turn to a market, a category or group of potential clients, in order to arouse an interest in the knowledge they can offer. They communicate ideas to the markets and point out problems, threats and opportunities that could be handled with their knowledge.

Your goal in this phase is to create an interest in your knowledge and confidence in your company, so that the chosen clients take the initiative to contact you. Doing this effectively means creating a demand for yourselves, which means that less effort will be necessary in the next phase, 'selling'. Peter Drucker comments, 'the aim of marketing is to make selling superfluous. Ideally, marketing should result in a customer who is ready to buy.'

Phase 2: Dialogue with potential clients about their specific needs

This phase is the process of 'dialoguing' with individual clients in order to induce them to buy your knowledge/product. It is sometimes called the selling phase, which Bruce Marcus describes as, 'an art that most professionals would rather stay away from because of its underlying implication that you're persuading people to do what they don't want to do, which ladies and gentlemen don't do, and is certainly unprofessional.' As we will point out in Chapter 5, the knowledge professional does not need to copy the art of traditional sales people. Promoting and persuading has little to do with successful selling in the knowledge-intensive business, where the ability to question, analyse problems and be a teacher is crucial.

Your goal in this phase is to obtain a mutual understanding of your potential client's problems, of the best possible strategy, and of the client's commitment to cooperate with you.

Phase 3: Collaborating to create optimal client value

This phase is the interaction with the client in a project. In this phase, the professional feels at home. It is now that the professional's competence is used to create maximum client value. Involving the client is a success factor in the knowledge business.

Knowledge quality differs from service quality. The values/results of knowledge are hard to measure immediately after 'delivery'. Consider a management development programme, an information system or a therapy course. The actual result/change is a process that has to take its time. Evaluation has to be made on a long-term basis.

In this phase the 'soft' aspects of service quality should also be considered, the quality that the client experiences in collaboration with the professionals and their company.

Your goal for this phase is to create optimal results for the client company and to make the collaboration a satisfactory experience for the client.

Phase 4: Follow-up and evaluating results

This phase is too often the forgotten phase. During the 1980s, consultancy services were bought and sold with levity. Too little attention was paid to evaluating the results (knowledge quality) of, for example, leadership programmes or information systems. The 1990s, in contrast, are the decade of learning through a focus on evaluation and feedback.

The fourth phase is more than evaluation. It also contains what is often referred to as 'customer care programmes', activities directed towards former clients in order to develop future business.

Your goal for this phase is to create a mutual awareness of the values you have created together with your client, to contribute to your own quality development and to encourage the client to remain in a mutually developing business relationship, acting as your ambassador.

CREATE YOUR OWN 'SALES DEPARTMENT'—FREE OF CHARGE

Knowledge companies seldom have sales people since their clients want to speak to experts/professionals. But they can create an efficient sales force around them which, furthermore, is free of charge— contented and committed clients.

Look again at the relationship circle in Figure 2.3. The outgoing arrows represent the clients who leave you and disappear from your circle of good relationships. We said earlier that the responsibility for implementing your knowledge remains with your clients, since they 'own' their problems. But if you consider the relationship and interaction between the clients and yourself in the role of consultant/specialist, the responsibility is on your side. Your ability to create and develop the client relationship is the marketing of you and your company.

Let us come back to the question of contented clients staying with your company and discontented clients leaving. If some potential clients refrain from your offer and leave the circle, it is a loss but still no catastrophe. The next station, though, is the critical one. A discontented client who leaves a good relationship after the collaboration phase is a greater loss than you could possibly realize. If a client leaves dissatisfied, what is likely to happen? Researchers have proved that although these clients may say little about their doubts or dissatisfaction to you, they will talk about it to others. On average, just one such client will spread dissatisfaction to eight people who, in their turn, will spread the negative news to their business contacts.

Image is not make-up—it is your real face. The image of a company, in the sense used in the advertising industry, is the sum of people's conception and evaluation of it.

The image of a knowledge company, unit or organization is primarily based on what people say about it, emanating from their own experiences of collaborating and/or communicating with the company, or from what they have heard others say. The image of the knowledge company is therefore analogous with its reputation.

Marketing of knowledge is not what you say about yourself. Rather it is the activities you are engaged in, the initiatives you take, the benefits and results you create, and the business relationships that you retain and redevelop to the benefit of your clients. Credibility is not the fruit of promoting yourself or your company: credibility and trust are created in the minds of the clients, based on their own evaluations and those made by other opinion makers.

So your company is promoted most effectively by contented and committed clients—based on the value you created for them.

THE KNOWLEDGE PROFESSIONAL'S TOOL KIT— THE SEVEN Cs

To be able to plan your business development, do your marketing and manage your client relationships, you need a few key words, or tools, to guide your thoughts. There are seven key words for the knowledge company, and they all start with the letter 'C'. Not surprisingly, we refer to those words and concepts as the seven Cs (see Figure 2.4).

The seven Cs:

- have been developed by us in collaboration with our clients;
- are designed for knowledge companies and organizations to use;
- are carried out by professionals themselves;
- are implemented through internal training and development programmes.

The first three Cs aim at activating your internal goal image. They are the cornerstones of your business idea for the whole organization, or for a single project. These Cs are: Choice of clients, Client information and Chain of client values.

The next three Cs guide you in activating the demand you want from your chosen markets and clients, through market and client communication. These Cs are: Contact network, Client education and Channels of communication.

The seventh C, Competence, actually also the starting point or origin (0), is the condition for present and future business, the investments you make in developing your knowledge for future business opportunities.

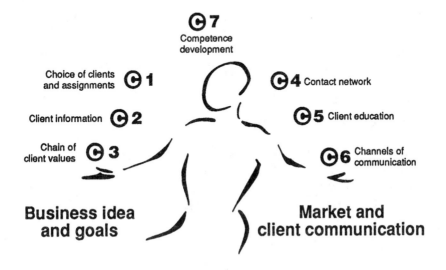

Figure 2.4   The knowledge professional's competitive tools

First C: Choice of clients

The first C deals with the goals you set concerning target client categories, ideal future business relationships and assignments.

Second C: Client information

Since your knowledge/product is adapted to the specific needs of chosen markets and clients, knowledge of your chosen client categories' situations, problems and needs is as essential as your professional expertise. To develop this part of your competence you need client information.

Third C: Chain of client values

The third C deals with the qualitative goals you set for yourself, focusing on client value and results. It also deals with how to use your clients' language in communicating this value to markets and clients.

Fourth C: Contact network

The fourth C deals with the target groups for your market communication, involving key people in the chosen clients' worlds, who can be helpful in obtaining client information and spreading your message and knowledge to your chosen markets, through their own forums and media.

Fifth C: Client education

The fifth C deals with how to choose and create messages in order to make the chosen markets and clients understand their needs and demand your knowledge. The implication is that people are interested in being given information that they consider useful in their jobs.

Sixth C: Channels of communication

The sixth C deals with all the channels you use for your client education, ranging from personal communication during activities such as education and seminars, to media such as papers, letters and books.

Seventh C: Competence development

The seventh C deals with your investment in future business opportunities, the learning and creation of new knowledge in line with your choice of clients and their future needs.

The following two chapters deal with the implications of the first six Cs. Chapter 6 deals with Competence development. The seven Cs are the cornerstones of your market planning process, for your company and for separate projects.

KNOWLEDGE PROFESSIONALS ARE BUSINESS DEVELOPERS

Knowledge professionals are not just marketers, they are business developers. They have no ready-made product to sell to a defined market. They have to discover new needs in old markets and constantly develop new knowledge to meet those needs. They also have to discover new markets for their knowledge and turn those markets into long-term client relationships. To market knowledge involves all professionals in a continuous process of:

- developing their knowledge base;
- identifying market segments which can benefit from that knowledge;
- learning about chosen markets/clients' problems and needs;
- contributing to the development of change for clients;
- creating an awareness of their activities, both internally and in their chosen markets.

ASK YOURSELF AND YOUR TEAM MEMBERS:

- What is the essential part of our offer? Products, services or knowledge?

- Do we use our knowledge to create optimal value for our clients and our own organization?

- How good are we at creating links between services and knowledge?

- Which of the four phases of the client relationship are we good at?

- Which phase(s) do we have potential to develop?

References

Christopher, Martin, Adrian Payne and David Ballantyne (1991) *Relationship Marketing*, Butterworth-Heinemann, Oxford.

Done, Kevin (1993) 'World Automotive Suppliers: Shockwaves keep coming', *Financial Times*, June 28.

Drucker, Peter (1973) *Management: Tasks, Responsibilities, Practices*, Harper & Row, New York.

Levitt, Theodore (1983) 'After the sale is over . . .', *Harvard Business Review*, September–October.

Maister, David H (1993) *Managing the Professional Service Firm*, The Free Press, New York.

Marcus, Bruce (1993) 'What are you?' The Marcus Letter, Vol 2, Issue 6, March, Newkirk, NY.

3

Visualize Your Goals

*'To fly as fast as thought to anywhere that is . . . you must
begin by knowing that you have already arrived.'*
Richard Bach

This chapter focuses on the three components of your business idea: Choice of clients, Client information and Chain of client values.

If you ask the leaders of a traditional industrial company about their goals and visions for the next five years, they will most probably answer in terms of profit, turnover and market share. However, if you put the same question to the managers of a knowledge company, you will probably be answered in qualitative terms. The managers will tell you what categories of clients they want to collaborate with and what types of projects they believe will provide most opportunities for development for the company and its professionals. Apart from sales and profitability being prerequisites for staying in business, they are also needed to develop and acquire new competence and business ideas.

These visions can only be made real through the energy, effort and high spirits of the knowledge professionals. The marketing of a knowledge company is the sum of those client relationships that are created, developed and retained by professionals.

As a result, management of a knowledge organization differs from that of a more traditional, hierarchical company. Instead of being run like a big ship with the captain giving orders from the bridge and the crew following them, a knowledge organization is like an armada of sailing dinghies each piloted by a professional. Every now and then the leader has to call the team ashore to discuss the common destination, which is the responsibility of each pilot to reach.

Destination and navigation are discussed together. As we have already discussed, the people working in a knowledge-creating company are not only marketers, they are business developers. Their role is to:

■   use their knowledge to identify groups of clients who can benefit;
■   seek out and analyse clients' needs;
■   translate those needs into value that can be created with their knowledge.

Formulating these elements in words means formulating your business idea. This chapter deals with those aspects of business development and marketing that have to do with the creation and understanding of your business idea.

Your tools are the following three Cs:

■   *Choice of clients*: your definition of target markets and preferred assignments.
■   *Client information*: market and client research and feedback.
■   *Chain of client values*: your understanding and definition of the results your clients gain from your knowledge or products.

FIRST C: CHOICE OF CLIENTS

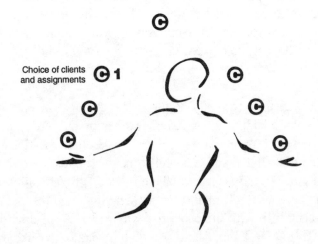

Choice of clients and assignments ©1

Visions and goals are essential to knowledge-intensive organizations. The first key to success is to choose, not to be chosen. If you sell a consumer product, it does not matter who buys it as long as you get your return. If people and knowledge make up your 'product', who you sell to becomes extremely important. The reason for this is that your clients play many roles in their relationship with your company.

'We shall be good for our clients. But that's not enough. Our clients shall be good for us too.' These are the words of a CEO of a consultancy firm addressing a seminar. Just consider for a while the implications of the collaboration between consultants/specialists and their clients. It is a highly interactive process where the exchange of knowledge between the two parties is the currency for creating client value and results. This chapter analyses what we can get and give through choosing the right business relationships.

Differentiating clients and customers

Services are customer oriented. People talk about the personal service given by, for example, a hotel or a department store. However, when looking more closely at personal service, you will find that it is not particularly personal. On the contrary, it is the role of service providers to keep a certain distance and not to put themselves in focus. Knowledge, on the other hand, is sold and produced in personal relationships and depends on the trust and confidence of both parties. This also means that an important dimension of the relationship is the sharing of values, attitudes and beliefs. This implies a personal relationship. As a result we refer to such customers as clients, to illuminate the implication of this stronger bond between the two parties as professionals and clients. Throughout the rest of this book, we will refer to the concept of client in relationship to knowledge marketing.

Clients' roles in relation to your company

What parts do clients play in the development of the knowledge company? What criteria does the knowledge-creating company use for strategic decisions concerning business, market and client development? Thinking through the intangible and tangible elements and benefits of a good client relationship is a means to activate the process of how to create a desired image with a major long-term impact (see Figure 3.1).

Co-producer
Creator of quality
Competence developer
Image creator
Ambassador
Potential business
partner

Figure 3.1   A client's roles

Clients are co-producers and creators of quality

If the service worker provides convenience for the customer, the knowledge professional has to involve and activate the client. As we said in Chapter 2, one of the success factors is involving the client as much as possible.

'We want competent clients' is the most frequent answer we get when asking for criteria describing 'the ideal client'. Clients have the responsibility for their own problems and development, and thus they are also co-responsible for the results that can be created through collaboration. The results you can create in terms of enhanced competitiveness for your client are as much dependent on the client's ability to make use of your knowledge as on your performance.

Clients are competence developers

Clients and projects are crucial factors in the competence development of the knowledge company. 'Projects are everything,' Tom Peters points out in *Liberation Management*, describing professional service firms as models for learning organizations. The firm David Kelley Design is cited as consciously using early/continuing client involvement in a structured way and only accepting assignments it can learn from. Working together with demanding clients and taking on assignments that mean a challenge to the specialists are the main ways in which knowledge companies can develop new knowledge.

Clients are image creators

You become associated with your clients and are affected by their image. In some professional fields the connection between business partners is very exposed, eg in advertising, auditing, architecture or criminal defence. Other fields, such as certain consultancy services or medical treatment, demand strict confidentiality from the professionals involved. Even so, clients are free to disguise their choice of consultant/professional/supplier—and they often do.

Being associated with well-reputed clients will give you a share of their reputation and trustworthiness and facilitates the decision process of future potential clients, who rely on the choices made by others whom they respect.

Clients can be ambassadors

Clients not only convey to others their choice of consultant; they also effectively spread their satisfaction or dissatisfaction with the assistance and advice they have received. The satisfied, committed client can turn into the most trustworthy ambassador and 'salesperson' you can ever have. A good measure of your quality is the rate of assignments emanating from recommendations made by former clients.

Clients can be business partners

New business ideas, services and products often develop as a result of client projects. A dynamic client relationship may be the key to new business ideas and projects if you ask yourself how something completed can be developed into something new.

Your client base—your invisible capital

A managing director once said about his company, 'Our largest fortune is not visible in the annual report.' Knowledge companies do not count their assets only in financial terms. In fact, their major assets are people: employees and clients. This view is mirrored by Richard Normann and Rafael Ramirez, who point out that, 'In an economy founded on the new logic of value, only two assets really matter: knowledge and relationships or a company's competencies and its customers.' In Chapter 6, we are going to deal with the issue of how to develop the professionals, the company's 'knowledge capital'. In Chapters 2–5 we deal with how to develop the 'client capital', your client base.

Divide your market into markets

The marketing of knowledge is marketing that takes place in the chosen clients' worlds, emanating from deep insights into the specific situations, problems and needs that apply to these business fields. This is called niche marketing (niche = appropriate place) and is the most effective way to proceed and succeed in knowledge marketing. Your best chance for reaching the clients of a specific market is to communicate with them in their own places, forums and media, eg in their associations, conferences and journals, together with their key people and opinion leaders.

Therefore, the marketing plan of the knowledge company is the sum of several marketing plans, one for each target client category. That is where the planning starts—in the analysis of present and potential categories of clients or business fields that could benefit from your knowledge. The process of dividing your market into categories is called market segmentation. Neil Morgan, lecturer in marketing and strategy at Cardiff Business School, has highlighted this issue: 'In simple terms market segmentation can be described as the process of breaking down a total potential client market into a number of distinct groups which respond differently in some important way to marketing programmes.'

Start by analysing your present client base

Having a clear image of the patterns of your present client base is the first step towards setting realistic goals. Your choice of strategic clients starts by being aware of your present situation. Start by dividing your current clients and projects into groups. Look for information that is relevant to your strategic discussions about client choice. Analyse patterns and what implications they have for the organization's future development.

Sort out your client list. Make a pie and cut it into pieces. A company could, for example, sort its clients in terms of:

- sectors of the economy (services, industrial, public, etc);
- business fields;
- professional fields;
- sizes;
- geographical location.

Possibilities for dividing the market of an internal unit include:

- levels;
- functions;
- groups with similar needs.

You could also divide your assignments and projects according to their percentage of your turnover.

Logica, employing about 3400 people, works internationally with information technology, supplying consultancy, software and systems integration services. It gives an account of the pattern of its client base in its 1992 annual report. It makes this analysis in percentages of turnover according to the following criteria:

- market sector;
- activity;
- client location.

Analysis by market sector   **Analysis by activity**   **Analysis by client location**

(Extract from Logica's 1992 annual report)

Logica also publishes its 'client capital' in terms of a client list, covering 281 of the world's leading organizations from nine information-intensive business fields. The annual report is built on the theme 'Winning together', indicating the strong bond between Logica and its clients and Logica's dedication to client value/results.

Your own process of defining your choice of clients continues with discussion and analysis of the interrelations you see in your present client base and assignments/services/products that you have in your 'basket' today:

- How does your company use its total knowledge to create optimal value for your clients and yourselves?
- How do you match your knowledge, services and products and how do you use them in your offerings?

This analysis is vital as a platform for developing strategy.

Divide up your projects/services/products as well, so that you can discuss the past and present state. Awareness of the present situation helps you to see the necessary changes that will influence your desired image, strategy and business plan. The following example illustrates how a consultancy redefined its business idea in terms of offerings.

A management consultancy firm analysed the patterns of its current and past assignments. It found out that it had too many assignments that were service oriented (analysis and report) and thus gave the clients too little help in the implementation of the advice. As a result it created new methodologies and extended its portfolio of offerings to clients with education and leadership development programmes.

Decide direction in terms of client categories

Knowledge marketing is long term. It may take years to become established in a new market niche. Starting up in due time, before your competitors, may be the difference between success and failure. The creation of a desired image continues with discussion of what you want your pie to look like in the coming years. This is the time to be visionary, but not without analysing the development of your market, asking yourselves such questions as:

- Have we discovered an increased demand for our knowledge/ products in some sectors or business fields? Could we be the first to enter that market and become established there before competitors do?
- Is competition in some of our present markets going to increase so that we must intensify our communication with them if we want to keep our position?
- Do we want to develop a new knowledge, which could be done through choosing a couple of pilot clients in a new market category or initiating pilot projects in partnership with present clients?

One example which illustrates the importance of choosing target markets strategically, is John R McKean & Co, a well-established firm of certified public accountants serving the greater San Francisco Bay Area.

John R McKean & Co offers a broad range of accounting, tax, management consulting and litigation support services to closely held businesses and individuals. Over the years the firm has developed an in-depth understanding of clients' requirements in specific fields such as:

- the legal profession;

- construction;
- real estate;
- financial services;
- transportation, with an emphasis on the bus and trucking industries.

Concentration on specific target markets makes it possible for John R McKean to offer solutions to a wide variety of problems facing these client categories. The firm uses an interdisciplinary team approach, in order to give every client the opportunity to enjoy the combined skills, experience, perspective and wisdom of the accounting, tax and consulting departments acting in concert.

One of John R McKean's client categories is small to medium-sized law firms. To this client group the firm provides not only tax and accounting services, but also law practice management consulting services for financial decision making in areas such as profitability growth, partner compensation, law firm strategic planning, billing and collection, accounting system design and reporting, in addition to expert witness testimony.

Through focusing on certain client categories, John R McKean is able not only to develop the knowledge necessary to meet specific client needs, but also to aim its marketing efforts towards these groups. As an example, in 1991, the firm put together a seminar for lawyers, 'Law Firms in Transition: Surviving and Prospering in the 90s', which highlighted a set of issues of specific interest to this target group. (You will read about the seminar in more detail in Chapter 4, under the heading 'Customer education'.)

Go on finding the 'plums'

Once you have decided on your direction, choose specific companies and organizations. This process starts with consideration of the 'ideal client' and the 'ideal assignment/project'.

Successful knowledge companies have the ability to think in terms of long-term relationship development. To activate a strategic outlook and the ability to prioritize, they frequently discuss their criteria of the 'ideal client'. Each organization has to find its own criteria for its preferred client and assignment. We can only share with you some of the criteria we have heard discussed by our clients.

Assessments of clients are made in terms of the following criteria. An ideal client company has (see Figure 3.2):

- a great need for our knowledge (means volume);
- good possibilities for success (means quality and good references);
- a high level of competence (means learning);
- profitability (means low risk);
- a good image in their own professional field (everyone knows who is 'best in the class' in their own field: working with such a client company means that you will share their reputation and image);

■ an extensive corporate network (widens your network and market possibilities).

Great needs
Good possibilities
High level of competence
Profitable
A good image
An extensive network

Figure 3.2 Ideal client company, example

One of our clients gave priority to the following criteria for their ideal client company. They should:

■ operate in an expansive business field;
■ be trendsetters;
■ have a long-term need for our services;
■ be able to offer challenging and developing assignments;
■ have a certain level of profitability;
■ carry on international operations and have an extensive business network (can recommend us, create new assignments and contribute to our own internationalization).

Your knowledge/product/offering to the market may be an important aspect of your client choice. If you sell data communication systems, a decentralized organization may be your ideal client. If you offer intercultural training, international corporations may be your choice.

One independent consultant has defined his target client company as having:

- low profitability;
- a certain size in terms of number of employees.

The knowledge he offers is internal development programmes for employees to increase their level of awareness of profitability factors!

Defining a couple of 'plums', ie preferred target companies, is a means of getting into their markets. If you see the goal clearly, you are in a position to recognize and seize the opportunities when they occur.

One day, for example, you may meet some representatives from an important target client company at a conference in which you are participating as a speaker. Bearing your company's goal in mind, you sit near these people at lunch and thereby create your first contact.

Qualify the people you want to collaborate with

Good results come from good cooperation. Likewise, ineffectiveness and unsatisfactory results are often as much due to the people who hired you as to yourself. However, before we discuss the qualities we appreciate in a collaborating client, let us focus on the concept of client. It is not an unequivocal concept. When practising their role as marketers, many knowledge professionals wonder: Who actually is the client? Your client may be a company or an organization, but which representatives of that organization should you communicate with? Who has the authorization to make the decision to buy your service/product? Who influences the decision process?

These are questions that are particularly applicable to staff units that are being reorganized into profit centres. Many parties are involved in the purchasing process:

- the buyer, initiating and preparing the purchase and selecting potential suppliers;
- the formal decision maker, the manager;
- the recipients of our knowledge/service/product (sometimes called 'users' or 'personnel');
- influencers, opinion makers, informal decision makers (eg specific specialists or union leaders).

All those parties, sometimes referred to as the buying centre, buying team or buyer network, influence the purchase and the result we can create with our collaboration. It is important to discuss the following questions:

- Who is the formal client, the decision maker?
- Whose errands do you run?
- What are the ethical principles that you use as guidelines in your client communication?

Remember that it is the client organization which buys your knowledge/service/product. Those who are responsible for operations, and have the formal authorization to make decisions, are your formal clients. On the other hand, you may have several target groups in your client's organization, groups or people that can be involved in your client communication. Such groups could include project team members, contact people and internal influencers, or 'gatekeepers'. It is an important long-term marketing strategy to broaden your contacts within the client organization.

Qualifying the ideal client/collaborator means creating a clear picture of the personal qualities and competences you appreciate in the people you work with in the client company. It does not mean that you must reject a client who is asking for help. On the contrary, you become more aware of what personal qualities are needed in the client in order to create results.

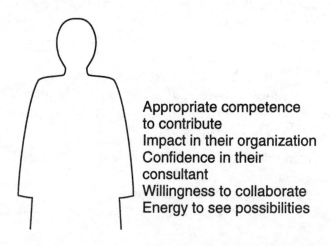

Appropriate competence
to contribute
Impact in their organization
Confidence in their
consultant
Willingness to collaborate
Energy to see possibilities

Figure 3.3   Qualities of ideal collaborators—an example

Ideal collaborators are often defined in terms of whether they have the following:

■ appropriate competence to contribute;
■ impact in their organization;
■ confidence in their consultant;
■ willingness to collaborate;
■ energy to see development possibilities.

Design for Business is a Zurich-based company specializing in corporate identity design and communication.

Its strategic choice of target client categories mainly includes internationally operating foreign companies based in Switzerland and small and medium-sized Swiss companies operating in local, regional and export markets.

Susan Ernst-Peters, owner and managing director, has formulated the company vision, which includes its choice of preferred clients and collaborators, in a strategy paper under a section entitled 'Philosophy and Values'. One of the objectives of Design for Business is to work with people who are visionaries, who aspire to be the best and reach the top, people who take calculated risks, who are international in their thinking, who want to make a global contribution, and who want to work with the best and most unique people across cultures and national boundaries.

The company's guiding star is formulated as follows: 'The best and most unique, for the best and most unique, with the best and most unique.' Through this it strives towards its goal, not to be the biggest, not to have the highest possible turnover, but to use its creativity and insights to add value to our world.

Saying no can save a lot. Discussions about your choice of clients hinge on outlining the strategy for the future direction of your marketing efforts and activities. The cost of marketing knowledge is defined in terms of professionals' time spent on information and personal communication. It is more important to do the right thing than to do things right.

A professional service company has no obligation to accept everyone wanting to be a client. Defining criteria for the non-client can be useful training that will often be worthwhile. Awareness of these criteria also keeps professionals from spending their time on the wrong prospects.

You may think this discussion is somewhat presumptuous. Perhaps you want to maintain that survival is what matters. We agree that you may not be able to reject an assignment, but you must at the same time calculate your risk. One of your most profitable internal discussions for the long term may be the one that aims at defining the situation, position and qualities your company demands from those organizations and people you are going to do business with. And vice versa: Who are we definitely going to say no to?

Summary

Choice of clients is the internal process of developing and formulating long-term business goals.

It means mentally creating a desired goal—a joint vision for all the professionals in the company to guide them in their everyday activities. Those managers and partners who constantly keep developing and activating a picture of target groups and target companies in the minds of their team members will most probably be more successful in reaching their company's business goals than those who leave them to 'chase whatever they like'.

SECOND C: CLIENT INFORMATION

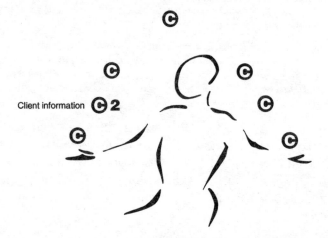

Client information

Every professional has to take part in market and client research. Since the business idea of the knowledge company is to help its clients to solve unique problems and initiate a change, the most important qualification—apart from professional expertise—is the ability to search for and analyse the chosen clients' situations and needs. The marketing that we deal with in the knowledge business has more to do with identifying problems and asking questions than with making propaganda and presenting arguments for specific products or ready-made solutions.

Knowledge companies are ahead of their clients, creating knowledge that may mean new possibilities for those who use it. Consequently, the marketing problem facing the professional is the lack of spontaneous demand. Potential beneficiaries are often unaware of the possibility of developing their competitiveness by new methods. Or perhaps they are unaware of the threats that will face them if they do not take certain measures and ask for professional help. This is the marketing challenge for the knowledge company. Those professionals who identify new needs and make potential clients discover them have attracted the interest of those potential clients. Therefore knowledge professionals must make forward thinking and anticipation their role and accept responsibility for the development of their clients.

As a professional in a knowledge company, you have to be constantly in the process of seeking, keeping and developing information about your chosen client categories—about their markets, business fields, customers, needs and possibilities. Let us briefly look at how you, as a leader or team member, can develop your company's marketing potential by seeking client information in each phase of the client relationship.

Market information

Marketing aims at arousing your chosen clients' interest in your knowledge and company so that they will take the initiative and contact you. This will only be possible if you can prove to them that you have an understanding of the specific situations, problems and needs of their particular business sector. In other words, you have to convey to them that you have a picture of the threats facing them and the possibilities they may have. If you are going to market your insight into your clients' needs, you have to have a good knowledge of those needs. In order to find the key to their interest in 'dialoguing' with you, you must make sure you have identified their needs before they do it themselves! This is done through continuous market and client research.

Create sources of market information

Seeking market and client information, creating business intelligence, is an essential part of the knowledge company's marketing process and the responsibility of each professional. The total amount of market and client information in a company is the sum of all pieces of information gathered by all professionals. How do you get started? The first step is to establish your sources of information. Think of one of your client categories—your target groups. Where can you find information about them and their market, situation and business?

All marketing begins internally! Start by finding out what information you can get from team members and colleagues. After that, step mentally into your chosen client category's world. Ask yourself: Where do they meet? What do they read? Who do they listen to? This may give you the idea of contacting their business association, professional association, or employers' association. From these you may receive invitations to their conferences and information about annual meetings and seminars, which will give you a fairly good overview of what is going on in their markets and business fields. You may find it valuable to attend some of the conferences as a participant. This will give you more information about what is going on in this field. The list of participants may contain some of your target clients and key people.

You may then find it useful to subscribe to your chosen client category's media, eg business journals, professional journals, newsletters. You could search in an external database or contact a library for additional information.

Another approach is to contact other consultants working with your chosen market but in other professional fields, or your chosen clients' subcontractors and suppliers. And do not forget to take the opportunity to put questions to a couple of your clients' clients, if you happen to run into them.

CHECKLIST: YOUR SOURCES OF MARKET INFORMATION

Internal information sources:

- team members
- colleagues
- internal database

External information sources:

- the chosen client category's business association, professional association, employers' association, conference organizers
- their conference and training programmes
- their business journal or professional journal
- trade journals
- other consultants working with this client category, eg accountants or management consultants
- suppliers and subcontractors of the client category
- public databases

- political decision makers
- researchers in their field
- the clients' clients, who could be users or consumers of services or goods

Organize your market information function

If there are any large-scale advantages in knowledge companies, one of them is the client and market information function.

Coopers & Lybrand is one of the world's three leading auditing groups, employing 67,000 knowledge professionals and service personnel. Understanding the client's business is an essential feature of its client service approach. As expressed by one of its partners: 'Without doubt, the single most important determinant of a successful client/service team relationship is the team's ability to provide solutions to the client's problems. How can we possibly be "business advisers" if we can't demonstrate to the client our knowledge of the business and the industry in which it operates?'

In order to provide its teams with the knowledge they need of specific industries, Coopers & Lybrand has created internal pools of expertise, 'industry groups', who provide the organization with 'business intelligence' through gathering, analysing and communicating information on specific industries.

Coopers & Lybrand's service teams can make use of these groups for expert input at the appropriate time. A lead partner describes how he used this market information in his group's work for a client in the retail business: 'At a recent team meeting we invited two members of the retail industry group. They made a short presentation on the industry issues, giving the team a context for our analysis of the specific problems facing the client. They were also able to contribute very effectively to our discussions throughout the day.'

The importance of this focus from the clients' points of view is maintained by one client: 'We continue to come back to Coopers & Lybrand for consultancy services because not only do they know us, they know our industry as a whole, and can advise us on how we compare with our major competitors.'

A small consultancy can organize its client information in a similar way, through making each consultant responsible for gathering, filing and communicating information on a specific business field, industry or market, thus making this consultant an internal expert on a specific target market. One small consultancy we know of keeps its market information, articles, research reports, brochures, annual reports, etc in files that are easily accessible to all consultants. The information is labelled and filed according to the firm's choice of client categories.

All professionals are part-time researchers

The role of knowledge professionals in relation to their chosen markets is to analyse and illuminate problems and opportunities, thus making the chosen clients understand their own needs. The capacity to seek, keep and use information about markets and clients' needs is crucial to any company wanting to be successful in the knowledge business. Whether it is a consultancy or an internal staff unit, the responsibility for this stays mainly in the hands of each professional.

In an article in *Management Europe*, Marion Devine refers to research carried out at an internal computer centre within Volvo's department for applied mathematics and statistics. The aim of the department is to help Volvo's business lines to shorten their lead times in areas such as production development. Results from interviews with engineers in the group were described as follows: 'The engineers who appeared to be high performers believed that their role was actively to seek out and solve problems. They achieved this through having extensive networks with people in other departments. In contrast, less effective engineers believed that the customer should identify the problem and then request help. The former group of engineers use their specialist knowledge to identify problems that no one else in Volvo is capable of recognizing.'

These professionals were good at actively seeking out and identifying problems that they could solve. As sources of information they used people with whom they had established mutually beneficial relationships (and gave information in return). They realized that they, with their expertise, had the responsibility and ability to take action. This we call proactive behaviour, which is necessary for success in knowledge marketing.

Knowledge marketing means more than waiting for orders. It means being your clients' 'guardian angel', taking initiatives based on your knowledge of their needs. In an article in *Sloan Management Review*, service researchers Parasuraman, Berry and Zeithaml refer to interviews they carried out with insurance buyers. Under the heading 'Customers Want Relationships' they quote customer opinions from the insurance business, describing the lack of initiatives from insurance brokers: 'They should be a partner and more actively give me advice on what my calculated risks are. When they are a partner our money is their money too' (business insurance customer) . . . 'Agents should come back to you and ask you if you need more coverage as your assets increase' (auto insurance customer).

Knowledge professionals creating optimal value for clients and their own companies are mentally and physically more in their clients' worlds than in their own. They are aware of their role as value creators and business developers and as such they constantly scan their market.

Mary Pitsy, executive search consultant and managing director of **Boyden Executive Search** in Brussels, is an excellent example of a proactive professional. She believes in long-term client relationships as a means of creating optimal client value: 'Knowing my client's organization and continuously following their development means creating an awareness of the problems and threats facing them, before they realize it themselves.'

Mary Pitsy is of the opinion that to be a professional does not always mean readily accepting your client company's definition of their problems: 'On the contrary, it means to be a bit uncomfortable, using your knowledge to present difficult questions and help them redefine their situation and needs.' She seeks information about the development of her client organizations through the media, through people in her network and, of course, through continuous contact with people in the human resource development functions of those organizations. She considers it her responsibility, as a long-term business partner, to contact a company when she suspects they will face a management problem, eg in an acquisition and merger situation or in a process of internationalization. 'You have to be there when they are changing and need you!'

Client development talks

Client information aims not only at identifying new business opportunities. It is your most important way of developing quality and learning. How often do you have an interview with your ongoing/present client with the aim of developing the quality and results of your collaboration? If your answer is 'never', at least it may be a consolation to know that you are in good company!

Most professionals refrain from using the most important source of information—the clients themselves. They do so in spite of the fact that the cost of getting a new client has been proved to be five times the cost of keeping a client. The most self-explanatory means of developing business information is seldom exploited. Only excellent professionals realize that their clients are not only their most important assets but also their most important sources of information for quality development.

A lawyer made it his routine to have a 'development talk' once a year with each of his regular clients. His intention is to investigate the client's view of their collaboration, making it possible to initiate necessary improvements, and to get a picture of the needs and expectations for the coming year. In order not to direct the client he starts with the question, 'What is important for you in our collaboration?'

In our internal development programmes, participants are encouraged to carry out client interviews. This is often the first time they have given themselves—and their client—the opportunity to talk about the business relationship, quality, and so on.

When reporting the results of the interviews, we usually ask the participants, 'What was the client's attitude towards participating in a talk like this?' We have never heard that they met with a negative attitude. On the contrary, clients want more interest and care from their business partners, and they regret that the usual interaction focuses only on ongoing projects. Many clients want to have such a talk at least once a year! In Chapter 5, you will read about how to conduct follow-up and development meetings.

Summary

Client information is the process of seeking information about target markets and clients, and analysing that information to find new needs for knowledge, products and services. It is also the process of following the development and situations of your former and ongoing clients in order to be able to 'be there when they need you'.

THIRD C: CHAIN OF CLIENT VALUES

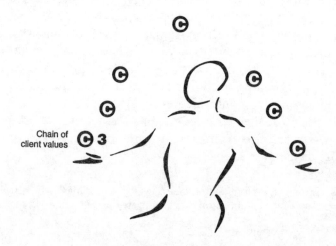

Chain of client values **C** 3

Through the process of seeking market and client information you enhance your picture of the problems and needs of potential and present clients. The greater the need, the greater the value you can contribute through your knowledge.

Knowledge buyers do not buy your methods, tools, service concepts or systems. They buy *results*. These results may be expressed in terms of money, time saving, efficiency, productivity, quality, etc. Even so, many knowledge companies still focus their marketing on their products, methods and techniques and cannot translate these into value for clients expressed in the language that clients want to listen to and speak.

All business fields have their own tools and means of production. The joiner has a toolbox but this does not mean that he starts demonstrating it to the customer who asks for help with the design of a new kitchen. The joiner focuses the discussion on the customer's cooking habits and outlines the features of the possible new kitchen he can construct.

Consultants, on the other hand, are too often fascinated by their tool kits and focus on them, 'packaging' their knowledge in terms of tools that will rarely be understood by people from other business fields and, consequently, not by clients.

We have looked at pamphlets and letters from three business fields. What they try to market is presented as follows:

- outsourcing, facilities management, shareware;
- equity swaps;
- benchmarking, TQM, business process reengineering.

Guess what business fields they represent!

Consultants also believe that clients interpret their codes in the same way that they do. Actually, our language commonality is considered to be at a peak when we leave senior school. As soon as we start specializing, the gap between different professional languages widens. For example, let us consider the word communication. What does this concept mean to an advertising expert, a telecom expert, a computer consultant, a psychologist, an actor, a journalist?

Client value is related to problems and needs

A key factor in preparing your marketing plan is creating an internal consciousness of the value the use of your tools/methods/systems creates for your chosen clients. Another key factor is expressing that value in the clients' terms and language. Since you work with change and the development of clients' competitiveness, you have to be concrete about what you are going to contribute to and how it can be measured.

Managers of a healthcare unit within a hospital stated in a seminar where we acted as facilitators that they wanted their clients (internal managers) to buy their programme for rehabilitation.

We pointed out that they had to find out what would be the customers' benefits from the programme. At the follow-up seminar they presented a chain of client value that was meant to explain their internal dialogue and their dialogue with clients about goals and results. They found that with a programme for rehabilitation they were able to contribute to the hospital's competitiveness by accomplishing:

- lower absenteeism;
- better teamwork;
- faster learning;
- better quality medical treatment;
- increased patient satisfaction;
- a better image for the clinic;
- enhanced profitability.

What this group of participants discovered through internal discussions about former experiences was how their activities in this kind of programme were related to preventing a chain of problems in the client's organization.

The chain of value that they contributed through their programme was directly related to the complexity of the client's problems and needs.

Make your client perform

A great deal has been written about service quality. One of the current key words in that context is 'performance', referring to the production and 'delivery' of services. This is not enough for the knowledge professional, who has to be goal oriented, having another performance in mind—that of the client. The goal of the knowledge professional is to make the client perform better. The consultant or professional is a contributor, coach, co-driver, inspirer, catalyst, educator, facilitator. The fact that the success of consultancies is measured in terms of profits earned in their own company is paradoxical, when the success should be measured in terms of their clients' profits and development.

'Successful change programs begin with results' is the title of a *Harvard Business Review* article by Robert Schaffer and Harvey Thomson. The authors emphasize the lack of goal-orientation that often characterizes change and development programmes. 'The performance improvement efforts of many companies have as much impact on operational and financial results as a ceremonial rain dance has on the weather.'

They conclude that results-driven programmes bypass lengthy preparations and aim at quick, measurable gains within a few months. Results-driven programmes set up measurable, short-term performance improvement goals, even though the effort is a long-term, sustaining one: 'Within 60 days, we will be paying 95% of claims within 10 days.' The mood is one of impatience: 'Management want to see results now.' The role of staff experts and consultants is to help managers achieve results, not to 'indoctrinate everyone into the mystique and vocabulary of the program.'

Three dimensions of value

Before you start reflecting on how you and your company express the results for the client and the terms in which you set qualitative goals, you might be helped by a short introduction to formal value theory, axiology (from the Greek word *axia* = 'value'). The originator of this formalization of the value concept was an American professor of philosophy, Robert S Hartman (1910–1973).

According to axiology, value belongs to one of three hierarchically ordered dimensions: intrinsic, ie soft value, within people; extrinsic, ie practical/functional value related to output and time; systemic value, ie financial value.

1. *Intrinsic value—soft, intellectual or emotional value.* Knowledge, capabilities, skills, personal values, attitudes, confidence, satisfaction, relationships, self-image, perceptions of jobs, culture, loyalty, etc, at an individual, group or corporate level.
2. *Extrinsic value—practical/functional value, having to do with output, time and quality.* Enhanced productivity, efficiency, quality, reduced delivery time, increased sales rates or market share, number of initiatives taken, tasks completed, time saved, reduced rate of absenteeism or product development time.
3. *Systemic value—financial value.* Yield, profitability, turnover, income, cost reduction, value added.

Value of the first kind is possible to measure and assess verbally and on scales. Value of the second kind can be measured and assessed by key figures (produced units per hour, rate of scrap, waste, rejects, rework). Value of the third kind can be assessed in absolute figures.

Applying formal value theory to the context of knowledge marketing gives you a means of discussing and analysing:

■ the patterns of your clients' problems and needs;
■ the value you contribute;
■ how different kinds of value are interrelated;
■ how you and your clients can measure your results/quality.

The understanding of the value you create with your knowledge does not develop easily. Most of the professionals we interview have little awareness of the value they work for, one of the reasons for this being the lack of follow-up and evaluation of results. Defining your chain of client value identifies the core contributions you make to your client's business. Having an insight into that value is essential for professionals' work and sense of self-esteem. A participant in one of our internal development programmes aptly remarked, 'We have to be convinced ourselves.'

Awareness of the value you create as a professional or with a high-tech product can only be developed through mutually trusting, long-term client relationships. Insight into client value is one of the qualities differentiating an experienced professional from a junior consultant.

If selling is your aim . . .

How do we apply the concept of value to the marketing and selling of knowledge? To create a demand for your knowledge/product you have to think beyond the 'deal'. You have to concentrate your mind, communication and client dialogue on the results that you can create together with them. Sales courses teach how to 'close deals'. For knowledge professionals, such focus will in fact counteract their purpose. Which client would not feel the self-interest and insecurity of a professional who imitated the traditional salesperson's way of presenting a product?

Professionals who are truly conscious of the results their knowledge/product has created for former clients can be self-reliant and able to focus the dialogue on the client's situation and need.

The client's expectations are your responsibility. Service management theorists stress the importance of satisfying, or even exceeding, customers' expectations. You can find hundreds of books and papers repeating this message.

The knowledge professional has to rethink—does this concept fit the marketing of knowledge? One essential difference is that the knowledge professional's clients often do not know what to expect, they may even be unaware of what their real problems are. For a simple service, like that of a travel agency, a restaurant or a bank, we all have clear expectations based on awareness of our needs and former experiences. But when investing in buying a professional service or a complex product the clients may have no former experience. How can they know what to expect? It is the responsibility of the knowledge professional to initiate the discussion about needs, goals and results. It is the responsibility of both parties to collaborate to achieve those goals and to evaluate results.

The international management consultancy the **ForeSight Group**, founder of the School for Intrapreneurs and developer of intrapreneurial management, is committed to results. Together with clients the consultants set up goals on all three dimensions of client value and follow-up in a 'Profit & Loss' assessment and a 'Group Learning Balance Sheet'.

Working on a development programme for The Body Shop during the spring of 1993, the ForeSight consultants identified the results the group of participants had reached 300 days after the start of the programme. The group had performed well and the value they had created for The Body Shop was summarized in a follow-up seminar:

- *Financial value.* Profit improvements of between £768,000 and £1,000,000.
- *Extrinsic value.* Four key improvement projects completed, seven well under way, 93 new improvement projects initiated.
- *Intrinsic value.* Vision, learning in change management, cross-fertilization, the feeling that 'we can do it, but it takes effort'.

The ForeSight Group regards follow-up and communication of results as the key to both internal and external understanding about what its services can achieve.

The Group has no brochure. Instead, it has a collection of letters, written by clients, who review and describe the values and results they have experienced and measured in their collaboration with the ForeSight consultants. The clients describe in their own words the chain of value that has been created by the ForeSight programme.

Sven Atterhed, partner of the ForeSight Group, emphasizes the importance of defining and discussing goals and results even if not all are measurable in figures. Evaluation of results in relation to goals is the platform for learning and developing the product/programme. It is also the platform that the clients need before they are able to buy the knowledge/product again and to recommend the consultant to their business contacts.

Measuring the unmeasurable

The business of training and development programmes has a tradition of evaluation. However, many trainers and HRD departments question the relevance of traditional evaluation. Dr Roger Poulet, management consultant and organizer of the European-wide PRC Consortium based in London, is not content with either the traditional post-course 'smile charts' or with concepts of long-term 'ultimate value' as simple estimators of effectiveness.

The former tends to measure little more than the quality of the food, while the latter is dependent upon too many other factors, both internal and external, for it to be an effective measure of training quality. In an article in *Training and Development Journal*, Roger Poulet and Gerry Moult emphasize that development training should aim at activating individual personal energy that creates a potential for action. This potential can be measured in terms of participants' intention to do things differently. It is the degree of conversion to this potential into new behaviours and actions in line with the company's goals that provides the measure of success or failure of training interventions.

Poulet and Moult have shown that the potential for action is closely related to participants' subjective attitudes and self-concepts. Their research shows that all programmes, from the exclusively technical and skill based to the developmental and conceptual, are mediated by the value systems, self-image, expectations and ambitions of their participants. And it is these factors which determine the level of identification, acceptance and implementation, ie whether people really will do something with what they have learned. Poulet and Moult claim that this is the missing link in the transfer chain, and that trainers disregard it both to their clients' and their own disadvantage.

Our conclusion is that this thinking can be applied to all knowledge-intensive businesses that work with the transfer of knowledge to enhance their clients' competitiveness. This implies that it is important for consultants to understand and work on both intellectual (objective) and emotional (subjective) dimensions. This can be expressed as follows: knowledge quality is the *result* that clients get, service quality is *how* they get it.

It is not only change/results that matter. Client collaboration has a soft side that is called service quality and that has to do with your organization, focusing on matters like accessibility, your telephone service and other aspects of communication, promptness, billing practices, etc.

Zeithaml, Berry and Parasuraman have identified five major dimensions of service quality, derived from extensive multimarket research and common for most business fields. The five dimensions are tangibles, reliability, responsiveness, assurance and empathy. By asking our clients, 'Which of these five service dimensions do you believe are the most important ones to your clients?', we obtained the following two priorities:

■ Responsiveness, the willingness to help customers and provide prompt service, eg accessibility of consultants, telephone service, etc.
■ Empathy, the caring, individualized attention provided to the customer, eg by secretaries.

In our view, current academic research on service quality is not appropriate for application to knowledge organizations and their client relationship. The practitioners have gone beyond the theory.

One country that has developed a tradition of quality surveys for professional service firms is Holland. It has, owing to a lack of natural resources, a small industrial sector but an extensive business service sector. For such a relatively small country, you will find a surprisingly high number of banks, accountancy firms and management consultants. Dick Weiss is managing partner of Weiss Strategy and Marketing Consultants for Professional Service Firms in Amsterdam, conducting research and giving advice to professional service firms. Dick Weiss relates that Dutch accounting firms make market and client surveys into joint activities with the advantages of cost sharing and large amounts of reliable data. Through joint surveys, Dutch accountancy firms have identified the most important aspects of an accountancy service's quality to be the following:

■ involvement of the accountant;
■ spontaneous advice;
■ price of the services;
■ promptness;
■ easy to reach;
■ punctuality;
■ expertise and quality.

Weiss describes research carried out in 1992: 'Very recently some firms carried out countrywide client satisfaction surveys with some shocking results. The respondents were asked to rank their accountants on a scale from one to ten (one being extremely unsatisfied with them, ten being more than satisfied). The average scores that medium-sized companies in Amsterdam gave their accountants ranged from 4.8 to 6.6, which should give some of them cause to get to grips with development of quality.' (In Chapter 5 you will read about Coopers & Lybrand's approach to their client service.)

When asked about his experiences of working with client satisfaction measurement (CSM), Dick Weiss gives the following advice: 'When carrying out customer satisfaction measurement clients are asked to make a rating on certain aspects ("promptness", "expertise", "involvement" etc) and to give an impression of their overall satisfaction. Remember to ask them for their *suggestions* to improve your service:

- use an external research organization;
- use telephone-interviewing (as opposed to postal);
- inform clients beforehand with a letter [in Dick Weiss' experience the percentage of no response drops to a mere 2 per cent];
- do research on a continuous basis, for instance yearly or every other year—the research should not be anonymous and this should be explained to clients; and, extremely important,
- follow-up, especially when a client shows dissatisfaction in any way.

'Failing to follow up is a sure way to lose clients. Clients expect that after they have listed their complaints, the consultant will take action to rectify them.'

Does CSM lead to results? 'Yes, for example: an accountancy firm, with about 6000 clients, found out that 212 clients had plans to change accountant within 12 months. These clients represented ECU 498,200 of fee-income.

'The firm spoke to all these dissatisfied clients and with the right measures, none of them very sophisticated, they were able to convince 138 clients to stay, "recovering" ECU 358,700 worth of fee-income. From the suggestions from clients to improve the services a lot of leads for additional business could be extracted, leading to proposals to already existing clients worth almost ECU 800,000.'

The importance of consciousness

In our work developing marketing competence through internal development programmes, we have learned that there is a strong connection between the ability to win and retain clients and a strong consciousness of client value. People who have identified their capacity to create change radiate that feeling and are better at creating confidence than others. The philosopher Joseph Campbell says, 'I have a feeling that consciousness and energy are the same thing somehow. Where you really see life energy, there is consciousness.'

Summary

The chain of client values is a concept that focuses your attention and communication on the results that you can create for your chosen clients. It is based on your insights into the problems, needs and business opportunities in each of the market segments that you have chosen to operate in. Your clients buy a result, not a method or an activity!

ASK YOURSELF AND YOUR TEAM MEMBERS:

- How do we analyse the structure of our present client base?
- How do we want our client base to look in three years?
- How can we keep informed about the new needs of our clients?

What are our best information sources?

- Through reviewing our presentation material, brochures and proposals, do we find that they communicate the methods and concepts practised by our company or do they focus on the problems we see in clients' businesses and on the value we can contribute to them?

References

Bach, Richard D (1973) *Jonathan Livingstone Seagull*, Turnstone Press Ltd, London.

Campbell, Joseph and Bill Moyers (1988) *The Power of Myth*, Bantam Doubleday Dell, New York.

Devine, Marion (1990) 'Is your knowledge base going to waste?', *Management Europe*, 3 May.

Hartman, Robert S (1967) *The Structure of Value: Foundations of a Scientific Axiology*, Southern Illinois Press, Carbondale.

Morgan, Neil M (1993) 'Market segmentation', *Professional Marketing*, Issue 4, Summer.

Normann, Richard and Rafael Ramirez (1993) 'From value chain to value constellation: designing interactive strategy', *Harvard Business Review*, July–August.

Parasuraman, A, Leonard L Berry and Valarie A Zeithaml (1991) 'Understanding customer expectations of service', *Sloan Management Review*.

Peters, Thomas J (1992) *Liberation Management: Necessary Disorganization for the Nanosecond Nineties*, Alfred A Knopf, New York.

Poulet, Roger and Gerry Moult (1987) 'Putting values into evaluation', *Training and Development Journal*, July.

Schaffer, Robert H and Harvey A Thomson (1992) 'Successful change programs begin with results', *Harvard Business Review*, January–February.

Weiss, Dick (1993) 'Where the professionals and liberals mix', *Journal of Professional Marketing*, Issue 1, March.

Zeithaml, Valarie A, Leonard L Berry and A Parasuraman (1990) *Delivering Quality Services*, The Free Press, New York.

4

Educate Your Knowledge Markets

'Knowledge is not knowledge until someone else knows that one knows.'

Lucilius, 125 BC

This chapter deals with the process of creating the right demand for your knowledge by educating your chosen markets. Using the three Cs of Contact network, Client education and Communication gives focus to the activity planning part of your marketing.

Stefan Witte, managing director of environmental company Adtec, says that 'A company's greatest asset is its demand.' As there is unlikely to be any spontaneous demand for your knowledge, a careful process is required to sell such intangibles. What you have to do is to teach the market to be a market and educate potential clients so that they become conscious of their needs and how they can become your client. The extent to which your company succeeds in creating a demand depends on the strategy you adopt. Your company's purpose is to create the right perception of your knowledge so that potential clients in your target markets obtain a comprehensive picture of its value and how your knowledge and ideas can be applied to their situations.

What we address in this chapter is a type of marketing that is not especially conspicuous or glossy. As a matter of fact, it does not even attract everyone's attention. And yet, when carried out in the right way, the right people seem to talk about just that particular company, their people and the area they work in. Everyone in the chosen markets seems to know about them and recommend them.

In the previous chapter, we discussed how to create the internal image of the value you can contribute. Marketing aims at activating that image in the minds of your target groups. Each target market should be addressed separately and in their own forums. It is now time to start the dialogue on your client's side of the fence. Your tools are the following three Cs:

■ *Contact network*: strategic contacts in the worlds of chosen client categories that provide you with information, confirmation and access to their forums. These people are the target groups you need to communicate with to reach the chosen clients. They are means of client communication.

■ *Client education*: transfer of usable knowledge that helps your clients to understand their needs and motivates them to develop a long-term business relationship with benefits for both parties.

■ *Channels of communication*: different ways and media you and your colleagues use for your client education.

You are a 'change agent', who expects your clients to commit themselves to develop, change, learn and act in order to become more competitive. As a knowledge provider, you are an initiator and motor in the process of your clients' development. This requires a certain amount of personal concern for your clients. Likewise, you have the right to expect energy and trust from them.

FOURTH C: CONTACT NETWORK

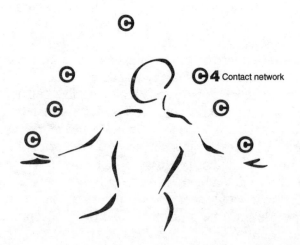

C4 Contact network

The most effective way of selling knowledge is to be recommended by a person whom the client respects and trusts. Surveys carried out by Zeithaml show that the majority of professional services are bought through personal recommendations.

Think about your own behaviour. How did you first hear about your doctor, lawyer, advertising company, financial adviser? Did you just glance through a pile of brochures or simply look up a list of names in a telephone book? Or was it over an evening meal with friends or a lunch with business partners that you learned whom to contact? Clients' trust in professionals' ability is not forged through reading expensive brochures. Their trust is built gradually through learning and reading the opinions of, for example, business leaders, 'gurus', other professionals, colleagues, etc.

As a result, knowledge professionals need actively to build up networks of strategic contacts in the chosen clients' worlds. Such contacts help professionals to transfer knowledge to their chosen markets. There is an inherent dilemma for knowledge companies concerning contact networks. Since every professional has his or her own contact network, when that person leaves the company, the relationships also leave. Seldom do other professionals within a company know the people an individual has been in touch with, about what and when. Yet it is mainly by and through personal contacts that the image of knowledge companies is built. Bearing in mind how valuable a contact network is in a knowledge-based company, in what way do you take care of this asset and transform it into capital? Who exactly owns the contacts? Your company or every individual professional?

In contrast to contacts, relationships cannot simply be transferred. What is important here is the information that someone in the company has a certain contact and relationship with, for example, someone who knows where knowledge can be obtained about a particular matter and/or knows who should be introduced to whom. Such information constitutes value for the whole company and as such it is an asset that warrants careful management.

How do you see your contacts? As a pack of cards to be shuffled every now and then? In fact, contacts are not something you can simply store, they are living relationships that need to be nurtured if they are to thrive.

Every knowledge provider in the company should actively use and share relationships with colleagues and clients in a mutually beneficial way ('Introduce me to Jim today and I'll introduce you to Jacqueline and Lawrence tomorrow').

Having a well-lubricated contact network and keeping in touch with everyone has nothing to do with PR (public relations). Attempts to reach as many people as possible, without involving them in any meaningful way, do not match the practices needed by knowledge professionals.

Effective contact networks need 'pruning' and 'weeding' at regular intervals, to keep them constantly up to date and ensure that they work for you when you need, for example, a recommendation, confirmation, knowledge transfer or information. Parallel to the changes made in your company, its choice of target markets or business idea, you also need to make corresponding changes in your network.

Business Week had a cover story by Martin Christopher, Adrian Payne and David Ballantyne entitled 'Relationship investing' about the role of network relationships and how companies can change to match the changes of their investors. They say: 'A relationship forms when an investor takes a long-term stake in the company. Then investor, board, and management talk regularly and monitor performance. Result: Companies get patient capital, and shareholders get management accountability and a better-run company.'

Four-leaf clover contacts

For a knowledge-based business, shareholders and clients represent just two target groups in its contact network. In order to ensure survival and development, your corporate communication needs at least four target groups. In their book *Relationship Marketing* Christopher, Payne and Ballantyne say, 'Relationship marketing strategies are concerned with a broader scope of external "market" relationships which include suppliers, business referrals and "influence" sources.'

In order to choose and categorize strategic people and contacts in a goal-oriented way, a 'four-leaf clover' model can be used (see Figure 4.1) in which:

- the first leaf symbolizes all your chosen *clients;*
- the second leaf represents the company's *'investors'*;
- the third leaf stands for the company's *suppliers*;
- the fourth leaf shows important *key people* in the chosen clients' worlds.

In order to reach or expand within a chosen client category's marketplace, you need to build up your strategic contacts in that particular category—ie its own four-leaf clover. You can also build a contact

Figure 4.1   Four-leaf clover

network for a project you are planning. When you have identified your network for each category/project, you then pile your clover leaves on top of each other.

You are then in a position to identify which relationships and contacts are the most strategic ones for your entire organization to develop. This analysis will assist you in prioritizing and allocating responsibility among your company's professionals.

First clover leaf contacts—Chosen clients

The first leaf (see Figure 4.2) represents people from previous, present and future client companies. Start by identifying the people with whom you should communicate within a client company.

Figure 4.2   Chosen client leaf

To avoid keeping all your eggs in one basket, broaden your contact network within that client's company by contacting people from different departments, specialist fields or management areas. They all need to know how exactly they could gain from your collaboration.

Second clover leaf contacts—Investor groups

These groups (see Figure 4.3) have a vested interest in the success of your company/project. Here you can include owners, shareholders, partners, team-members, managers, members of the board, business partners and associates who have invested their money, time, career or reputation. Analyse which 'investors' can help you reach and expand your chosen client category or succeed in a project.

Figure 4.3   Investor leaf

Third clover leaf contacts—Suppliers

Suppliers include representatives of your bank or computer company, computer consultants, auditors, printers or travel agencies. Their perception of your knowledge, methods and specialist competence is mirrored in their relationships with your clients or other people in your clients' world.

Suppliers

Figure 4.4   Supplier leaf

If they do not believe in you and your business, or have only slight knowledge of it, they may be making 'wrong' statements about you to your clients or in your clients' worlds. Furthermore, if they fail to supply you with adequate advice or the type of services or products needed for running your business, they can also adversely affect your performance.

While helping a computer company with a client survey, one of the clients interviewed informed us of an independent consultant who often worked for the computer company but who spoke badly about them. He did not have the right knowledge about the computer company and their consultants. Due to his lack of information and communication, the independent consultant constantly questioned the knowledge, experience and methods of the company. The client gradually lost confidence in the computer company and became doubtful about its capabilities.

When you choose suppliers or business partners for a project, you are also choosing your own quality and the possibility of a certain reputation and demand. This necessitates having a policy about:

- the standards you expect from your suppliers or business partners;
- how you interact with them;
- how you inform and involve them;
- what questions you put to them;
- how you let them be your sources of information.

Fourth clover leaf contacts—Key people

The fourth leaf (see Figure 4.5) symbolizes people who control media and forums in the chosen client categories' business environment and have the knowledge and possibility to help professionals build contacts in that environment. This leaf is the link to the client's side of the fence—to the world of the target market and chosen client. Through these strategic contacts in the clients' business environments, professionals gain information and access to their communication media.

Figure 4.5   Key people leaf

The Norwegian computing centre **Norsk Regnesentral** is an applied research organization employing about 100 research scientists working with, for example, estimation of oil reservoirs for oil companies and estimation of whale stock for the Norwegian government.

The company wanted to reach the international research market and identified the European Community Research Programs as an important platform for contact with potential clients. In order to establish a relationship with this key forum it made itself useful. With its knowledge of groupware technology the company developed, on its own initiative, a concept of communication and cooperation between project participants for different areas of application, such as medical diagnosis or oil platform troubleshooting. The result was a prototype called Global Window, the application of which led the company in contact with international clients and assignments at a value of $400,000 the first year—a good return on an investment of $50,000!

The process of building key people relationships starts by thinking, 'What's in it for them?'—ie what do your key people gain from these contacts? You need to plan and make your knowledge useful. Relationships cannot be one-sided, they have to be reciprocal. Perhaps you have an idea they can benefit from, or knowledge they can pass on which will strengthen their own position and reputation. For example, you could take an active role in your client's business association, assisting its management (your key people). You could initiate a conference with them or write an article in their newsletters and/or business journals. Become involved in the issues that are pertinent to your key contacts to help inspire them. You could also institute a prize together with a key forum.

A management consultant identified computer companies and computer departments as an important client category. Their 'hub' (and his 'key') was a local computer association and its members. He contacted its management about an idea he had which would benefit both the society and its members. Together the consultant and the association selected a subject for a conference which he was to help organize and give a presentation at. The conference was a success and together they decided to organize another. Since that was also a success, they now regularly offer courses, all of which are well attended. Through these conferences and courses, the consultant obtained several clients and assignments as well as a well-established reputation. Furthermore, the computer association has, for several years, gained considerable profits.

Summary

Contact network represents those people you develop as strategic contacts in order to get access to the clients' media, forums and opinion makers.

FIFTH C: CLIENT EDUCATION

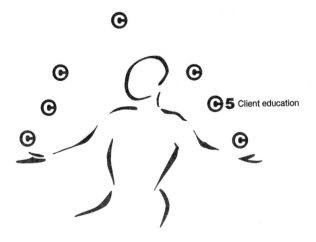

Ⓒ5 Client education

Do you know that your Sunday morning newspaper gives you more written information than an eighteenth-century person ever received during a whole lifetime? We are all confronted daily by an enormous barrage of messages, information and knowledge—both at work and at home.

The challenge for a knowledge-based business is not to break through this 'tidal wave' with tricks, sensational moves and messages like 'We are world-leaders' or, 'We offer perfect solutions'. It simply is not worth trying to present your potential clients with a simultaneous summary of all the knowledge and ideas encompassed within your company.

Client education means getting the attention of your chosen client categories, helping them to understand their situation by giving them new knowledge. To do this, professionals need to formulate messages that attract their chosen client categories so that they want to be involved—because they will benefit. Such messages will be coveted instead of thrown away and they will be transferred from person to person, since they have a value. We have often witnessed how companies and organizations have shared their knowledge through seminars, booklets, documents, etc and how they are subsequently contacted by potential clients with which they have never previously been in touch. These companies and organizations turn their client categories into missionaries, who help them to arouse demand for their knowledge.

Give the client a chance

Unfortunately, when many knowledge-intensive organizations address their clients they presume their clients are eager to consume all the 'important' information they give. Such organizations believe that clients discover information, want and understand it immediately and are able to translate and apply it to their own situation. They also expect clients to understand their needs and to be able to express their demand spontaneously. They never give the client a chance!

John Graham says in *Marketing News*: 'In the decade ahead, the biggest challenge for companies will be to retain and cultivate customers through education programs . . . Our goal is not to make sales, but to make customers. We view education as a primary responsibility. As a result, when we meet with prospective clients, they know our ideas, our viewpoints—our philosophy . . . An active program will constantly seek out new prospects who can become exposed to our message. That's both the task and the goal: keeping

the pipeline filled with potential customers who are drawn even closer
to your company over a period of time.'

A knowledge-intensive company's responsibility lies in helping
their markets to understand their needs through educating them. Such
a company should help their clients gain more understanding of their
situations and needs, possible solutions and the consequences of
enabling them to make wise and efficient decisions. To create a client's
consciousness is to gain a competitive demand.

We have seen knowledge organizations do this and watched their
markets expand as a result. We use the client staircase (see Figure 4.6)
to describe the steps and process clients and markets need to go
through to gain insight into their needs and to understand them.

To buy your knowledge, your client proceeds through several steps
which have to be 'climbed' together with you. Your role is to be there
to support and guide your client up to the next step. You have to start
at exactly the level they themselves are at. So do not force them, and
give them time.

The steps in the development of a client's decision to buy your knowledge

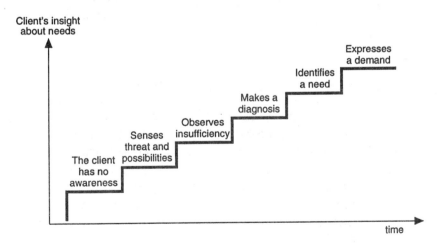

Figure 4.6   The client's staircase

Formulating your message

Clients are initially most interested in their own situations and possibilities and how they can develop them. Presenting your company's knowledge and services comes during the next step. Your aim is to move your client's point of reference forward. So how should you present your message? You could, for example:

- give your view of the client category's situation and needs;
- point out trends in your client's business world;
- give advice;
- debate and share values;
- illuminate connections;
- activate crucial issues;
- give 'early warning' signals;
- write reviews and summaries.

Whatever you do, your clients have to feel that you are on their side, that you stand up for them and are fighting their cause as their 'guardian angel'. As one consultant put it, 'Being with and making our clients see that we can help them to be profitable and make them profitable, will make us profitable.'

It is not necessary always to be the one who provides all the knowledge alone. You could collaborate with other consultants, researchers and scientists, clients, suppliers or others who have developed core competence within the area concerned.

The San Francisco CPA firm of **John R McKean & Co** (referred to in Chapter 3) chose law firms as its target market. It therefore highlighted a set of important issues of interest to law firms, collaborating with others in providing knowledge.

The firm began planning an educational seminar by selecting the target audience. Before the seminar it researched into what works and what generally does not work. On the basis of these findings, it acknowledged the value of an outside co-sponsor.

As the seminar was intended to be for non-clients addressing a broad subject matter, the firm saw it as important that there should be outside speakers with significant reputation and expertise. That is why the editor and publisher of the *Recorder*, a local legal newspaper, was invited to moderate the event. The agenda covered the following themes:

- 'Contemporary Directions in the Law Firm Environment', featuring a consultant from a well-known national consulting firm as speaker.
- 'New Directions in Practice Expansion', with a partner from one of the client law firms as the featured speaker.
- 'Improving Firm Profitability and Positioning for Growth', presented by a respected management consultant and friend of the firm.

- 'Compensating Partners', featuring John R McKean, the managing partner of the firm.

After two months of planning, attendance exceeded all expectations—both in terms of numbers and calibre of participants. The seminar had fulfilled its purpose of projecting the firm's expertise to the legal community, thereby enhancing its reputation as a leader in the field of law practice management.

It is still, two years later, reaping the benefits of this seminar by continuing gaining new clients at a slow but steady pace, and by enjoying continued working relationships not only with seminar participants, but also seminar speakers.

So forget information about your own abilities for a while and go in for transferring usable knowledge. Give your future clients an aperitif of knowledge.

Twice a year a children's hospital arranges public seminars for parents and people working with children. In the spring the hospital has courses about such areas as skull injuries caused by cycling, allergies and sunburn problems. In the autumn the seminars are about snow, ice and car accidents. So if your child is hurt you know what hospital is best. This hospital has shown its ability by having the right kind of knowledge as well as concern for children—by teaching one of its target groups how to prevent accidents. The seminars are advertised in parents' magazines, daily newspapers and in papers for people working with children.

In *Professional Marketing,* Neasa MacErlean says about the accountancy firm Vandenburghs, 'Many professional firms try to hide their expertise for fear of being copied. But Vandenburghs are very open in their knowledge—as in the way they help audit clients to understand their accounts better.' They see no point in having corporate brochures; instead they have written a book on the subject, which they hope will stimulate interest from potential clients. Vandenburghs have also helped to drum up local business by inviting local business representatives one evening to a get-together to see if they could assist each other—a way of creating valuable networks for prospective clients' communications.

Different categories of clients have different needs, ways of thinking, professional languages, business environments, worlds, etc. Use your empathy and try to figure out how they want to be approached, on their conditions, in their language and with their values. This means that you have to address one client category at a time, not all together, and thus respect their different needs.

Give an insight into possibilities

An educational approach can also be used in your dialogue with individual clients to present your message and to educate them about the benefits to be gained from your collaboration.

When you meet your potential clients face to face, they really look 'through you' if you do not apply your knowledge to their specific situation, if you do not bother to speak their 'language', or if you do not understand how they think. Ideas based on guesses and assumptions will discourage a client company from investing in your knowledge. Why should they when you show no interest in investing in them? Your client needs a specially mixed 'punchbowl' of your knowledge and a vision of what is going to happen during and after your collaboration. Clients also have to be involved in the process of 'making the assignment' as they have a special interest in the result.

During this process—which can sometimes be a matter of years—do not give up! Try to provide your client with value through your knowledge, bit by bit and step by step. Give ideas, discuss present and future issues. Believe in client development and show your commitment. Even the client who is not ready to give you an assignment could be your missionary. There are no short cuts: the key to success is carrying the relationship through.

Geotronics, a measurement technique company, entered into competition with Japanese and Swiss companies for an American army assignment. Geotronics knew it had a technical and scientific advantage; it just had to make the purchaser aware of it.

Its first contact with the army was in 1986. In order to continue this contact and render it more effective, Geotronics enlisted help from an American consultant. In 1993, after seven years of transferring knowledge and creating networks of contacts, Geotronics got the assignment and the American army changed its supplier after 40 years. The cost for meetings, information, transfer of knowledge and invoicing totalled almost $200,000 over the 7 years. The assignment was for $6.1 million.

How much knowledge can you share?

It may seem paradoxical to professionals to transfer the knowledge that is the source of their livelihood, and yet this is the only way for clients to get some idea of what is 'hidden' inside the head of the professional. It should, however, be valued and not just thrown away like 'pearls before swine'. If you do not value your ideas and knowledge yourself—who will? Express your professionalism to your clients and value the result of your effort.

> A PR consultant told us the story of his failure in transferring knowledge. He was approached by a company that was unhappy with its present PR company and wanted to find a new one.
>
> He arranged a meeting for an exploratory discussion with the company. During the meeting he asked the client questions which turned the client's world view upside down and challenged most of the assumptions the client had made.
>
> By the end of the meeting they had numerous sketches and the dialogue moved the client to think about the situation from an entirely different view and in a fruitful way. The consultant had helped the client translate an idea into its own business context to enable it to develop concrete steps or projects that would help it achieve its communication goals. On the basis of this meeting they agreed that the consultant should make the client a proposal. At a second meeting, they discussed this proposal which led to the identification of a series of projects. However, there was still no formal agreement on terms of payment, etc. The client now wanted the consultant to produce a 'test' and he finally agreed to do so. After receiving the test, the client manager requested a meeting at which he expressed his total disappointment.

Where do professionals draw the line in terms of input (before payment starts to flow) before the client finally agrees to sign and begins to pay? When do they decide to pull out of long preliminary discussions and how do they communicate this to the client without damaging image and reputation?

In an era when knowledge is 'panned' like gold and competitors and clients are in pursuit of the 'know-how nuggets' of new business opportunities, you must have a policy for your knowledge capital.

Julian Gresser, practising international attorney and president of JG Enterprises, San Francisco, has extensive experience as a lawyer, businessman, adviser and systems developer in the area of transcultural negotiations. He has also carried out research on invention, discovery and creativity.

Gresser maintains that professional knowledge has to be shared and transferred—and paid for. 'People don't evaluate what they don't pay for. Knowledge and know-how has to be priced in relation to the value it has for the receiver. The receiver of the knowledge shared must perceive it as an investment, not only in terms of money saved or earned. Our task is to help the other party discover their gain in time, effort and emotion. If the buyer of our knowledge does not have this perception, they will devalue (misprice) what we offer. Although there are times when for tactical reasons we offer knowledge "for free", if we give useful knowledge away unconsciously without compensation, it suggests a breakdown in our integrity which others will recognize and take advantage of.'

Knowledge professionals have to set a price on the knowledge they offer, for example a presentation, a paper or a report, or consciously consider other forms of compensation, ie the value of being written about in a business journal or being listened to in a major conference. Market education, performed in the right way, means 'client-financed' marketing in several steps such as a mini-seminar, pilot study or course.

Create a movement

The educative approach can be used not only for business develop-ment. Associations, movements and non-profit organizations work to create a change in values and patterns of behaviour, the basis of which is enhanced knowledge. The more you know about a problem, eg an environmental or medical problem, the more you are prepared to form your own opinion and take action to change the situation.

The Natural Step is a consensual approach to environmental issues, initiated in Sweden and being transferred to other countries including Great Britain and Poland. Unlike campaigning, where people are pressured to follow a particular course of action, the Natural Step works by educating its 'market'—the whole of society—in the relevant core knowledge which can be used as a compass to guide future plans and decisions. This approach respects the individual's specialist know-ledge and has motivated widespread participation.

A network of scientists created a consensual document as a basis for educational activities, which led to 16 new professional associations 'for the environment' and finally to training programmes for managers and executives, which provide the funding for the educational projects. The Natural Step initiates collaborative projects among major industries, local authorities and the professional associations, who all share the same core knowledge.

This results in the development of environmentally advanced products, popular environmental awareness festivals and shows on TV, the publication of books, radi-cal new strategies by large corporations and increasing public commitment to more responsible lifestyles.

The activity plan for the British group 1994/95 includes measures to educate its market:

■ publishing a Natural Step book in English;
■ training of 'catalysts' to guide pilot projects and professional networks;
■ writing a business plan for public education projects;
■ preparing training material for businesses and local authorities.

Through the educational approach, quibbling about isolated environ-mental issues is replaced by agreement on the basic conditions for sustaining health and economy and a decentralized potential for action. This can be compared with Greenpeace which takes a more provocative approach and carries out activities as a service for its 'clients'/members.

Corporate image—give facts about your company

Image is comprised of people's *knowledge* about a company and their *attitudes* towards it. Image is one of the company's essential intangible assets. In knowledge-based businesses these assets tend to be more important when another company has to estimate their value and form an opinion about its prospective business partner.

The traditional way of measuring and describing assets in the annual report reflects a company's past performance and says little about the future, although that is what the client is going to invest in. Giving facts about intangible assets such as:

- client satisfaction and results created for them (can be measured annually);
- professionals' skills;
- investments made in competence development;
- share of 'new' clients as compared to 'old' (can be given annually);
- investments made in marketing;

will give a more complete and exact picture of a knowledge-based business than strictly financial and organizational descriptions.

Frank af Petersen and Johan Bjurström point out the importance of correctly evaluating a company's intangible assets. They say, 'Current accounting practices and management information systems leave a lot to be desired when it comes to evaluating a business or predicting how an organization will be able to cope with the future . . . areas— often loosely defined as a company's 'soft capital', 'knowledge capital' or 'intangible assets' are increasingly seen as the decisive issues that distinguish a future winner from a mediocre player or worse . . . An acquirer should focus on the quality of the human resources, not just the numbers.' These aspects are as relevant to prospective clients as to acquirers.

Summary

Client education is the process of identifying what needs the target markets have for knowledge and deciding what knowledge is usable and should be transferred, to which groups and when. Through this approach, knowledge-based organizations create their own demand and image.

SIXTH C: CHANNELS OF COMMUNICATION

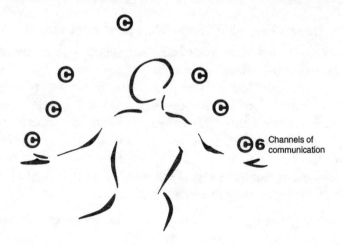

Channels of communication

Time is a very valuable factor for professionals. Therefore you need to be strategic and selective in how you communicate with your markets. You need to make the most of your opportunities and not let them pass by without personally participating in them. Knowledge providers need to be fully conscious of which professional should be seen and heard, at what places and in which forums in order to gain a certain goal. Communication is about finding a chain of opportune occasions as a frame to your core message.

Since it is personal relationships you are going to establish, you have to find your own way of doing that. The main media your company have are yourself and your colleagues. Therefore there are no limits to your marketing, apart from those you determine.

One keystone that Patrick Forsyth lays about media in his book *Marketing Professional Services* is, 'All are relevant and important to professional services . . . everyone in the firm is involved, everyone needs to adopt the right attitude and many will have specific roles to play.' Knowledge-based business communication does not originate from brochures, pamphlets, advertisements, etc, it starts with the knowledge providers themselves, their personal activities, such as making presentations, or writing articles and papers. Written or printed material they personally give away is a learning aid to the client more than a selling aid to the specialist.

Remember that one time is no time. Build a chain of different activities to form your dialogue and communication with your client. This chain must also help you in the process of anchoring ideas and creating confidence. The media for your dialogue is your choice, the aim of communication is to share a message with others. Do it the way you would like to be treated yourself.

The German professor Dr Gertrude Höhler points out the necessity of interactive customer relationships and the importance of looking at products and services through the eyes of the customer. She asks, 'What have you done for your customers today? . . . To be able to do something for our customers we have to spend our time together with them . . . Communication is the "boiler" in every partnership . . . What is good for the customer is also good for the company.'

She stresses that companies today have to take the step from marketing to marketing communication in order to develop their most effective future business together with their customers.

> A construction service company started publishing a small pocket book—'How to avoid the ten most frequent building problems'—at exactly the right time. As the building industry was suffering problems at that time, there was an immediate demand for the book. Technical journals wrote about it and consultants from the construction company were asked to give lectures. The need for knowledge was huge and the company started a school of its own and produced a series of compendiums on the subject. The business association contacted the construction service company and wanted the compendium series to be sent to all its members, one of the company's client categories. And the assignments kept on pouring in, even though this particular construction service company had no presentation brochure and did no advertising.

Again it is an advantage if you have the ability to put yourself in your client's situation when making the choice between different ways of communication. Choose those which are the best for you and your clients. Do not copy everyone else, find your own way to achieve an optimal dialogue.

Think of whom you are addressing, and when. Let the goals you set for the dialogue determine your choice of media.

The media that will create demand

A great deal of your market communication is done together with, or through, your identified key people, key media and key forums. The 'keys' should really be your door openers—helping you to choose the most important messages and helping your clients to an understanding of their needs and connecting your company with those needs.

As a knowledge provider, you could, for example:

- Be a member of your chosen client category's business association, or at least be on its mailing list, sharing information and taking part in the same activities as your clients.
- Initiate, arrange or take part in an event, a conference, a seminar or a course, and give a talk or a lecture, be the teacher or a member of a panel. If you do not manage that, at least be a participant in your client's events, stand up, introduce yourself and ask a good question, one you have prepared in advance. Take an active part! Invite yourself, do not wait for an invitation. Go and knock on their door; stop wondering why no one ever knocks on yours.
- Contact journalists, initiate articles, write your own advisory article, take part in debates by writing a topical article, and use copies of the article as presentation material.
- Institute a prize together with a client category's key organization and initiate sponsorships, surveys and research for the same purpose.
- Advertise news and facts about your company and its knowledge providers.
- Write a booklet, paper, compendium or other kinds of teaching aids. Perhaps a key organization will be interested in doing this together with you.
- Write letters, perhaps to those attending a conference where you gave a presentation, or to those who did not attend the course you invited them to, giving them a summary of the information given.

Whatever you choose to do, remember again that one time is no time. If you choose to take part in and give a talk at a seminar, it is not only the seminar that should be the bearer of your message. There should be communication activities both before and after the event. Ask yourself, in what way can I:

- have a dialogue with my fellow talkers so that they will get a picture of my knowledge area and my company?
- use the invitation to the seminar?
- keep in touch with those who attended my part of the seminar?

Make your own communication chain with the seminar/conference as one of the links—not the only one. It has taken you both time and effort to take part in the seminar, make the most of it!

One company which really leveraged its chain of communication is **Boyden International**, founded in 1946, established with an international network of 50 offices in 35 countries and one of the pioneers in the executive search profession.

Boyden identified an important future target market in Eastern Europe. In order to arouse interest in the subject of management resources in that area to both Western and Eastern clients, Boyden took the initiative to organize a conference— Management Resources in the USSR and Eastern Europe. They made the subject into a knowledge 'hub' and the conference one of the channels of communication. Prior to the conference, they created another communication 'spoke'. This comprised establishing strategic contacts with key people—with leading people from the USSR and Eastern Europe, including specialists from international branch organizations and international companies. In all 17 experts formed a 'faculty' who were also speakers at the seminar.

After the conference another channel of communication was produced, a report summarizing the conference briefly, and sent to all participants and other business contacts known to have a particular interest in the developments in Eastern Europe and the USSR, together with a 'personal' letter. Several follow-up communication 'spokes' were created by the Boyden consultants themselves when coming back to their local markets. These spokes consisted of articles, interviews, debate articles, etc in a variety of business newspapers, business journals and other important media. The consultants also wrote letters to their contact network reminding them of their involvement in the subject and describing the progress made.

All these channels of communication, or chain of communication activities, have established Boyden as *the* human resource company for the former communist bloc. They are now focusing and developing a new target area in a similar way— China.

Media for client dialogues

During the face-to-face dialogue about client needs, your media mainly focus on helping you and your client to anchor the ideas you have arrived at, and continuously building your client's confidence in you.

In this phase, too, look on communication as a chain of interrelated activities which will lead you into collaboration with your client.

As a knowledge provider you could, for example:

- Visit your client to initiate a dialogue. Remember when planning the visit that the focus is on your client and that business, not on you and your business.
- Invite people from your client company to visit your company. What will they see? And will they understand what they see? Think of the values you should be signalling and how to do that when your client comes to see you. Do not expect the client to be eager to visit you and see your business until they know that you are able to achieve results and both of you are ready for collaboration.

■ Use pamphlets and teaching aids and make presentations that concentrate on your client's needs, not on yourself or your business. Ask yourself, does the company presentation we normally perform at a customer meeting open the way for communication with this particular client and give an idea of our ability to help with exactly their unique need?

■ Use compendiums and other aids for your client's internal anchoring process. These are probably more important than a colourful glossy brochure.

Often you meet one or more people from the client company in a series of meetings. They get to know you, your ability, your knowledge area and your company rather well. But in what way do you prepare them for and help them in their internal anchoring process? What do they need that you could provide them with, when they are back in their own organization, trying to sell the ideas that you gave them?

Media that involve the client in collaboration

The client is a part of the final result and it is therefore necessary to actively involve them somehow. This responsibility is yours, not the client's.

As a knowledge provider, you could for example:

■ Use proposals and offers as bearers of knowledge, roles and expectations. Such documents define an assignment and form the base for your follow-up and feedback. They are not only legal and financial documents, they are part of your communication.

■ See invoices as an excellent instrument for giving the client a receipt for what they have purchased so far. This document should be clear and the client should not doubt for a second what it covers, what all the minutes and hours they have bought have led to or were used for.

■ Have stop points during your collaboration and sum up these points in contact reports, providing opportunities for mutual reflection and for harmonizing the project with the ambitions described in the definition of the assignment or proposal. These points also serve as your opportunities for straightening out, perhaps with the help of the client, complaints, hesitations and further thoughts.

■ Make reports compiled during the collaboration useful to your client and bearers of your knowledge.

Media for follow-up

Many companies conduct client surveys, mostly by post. In a knowledge company, this is not sufficient: the knowledge providers themselves have to dare to ask their clients about the results of the collaboration. This is personal communication after the assignment, aiming at establishing a long-term relationship, not fishing for short-term results. For example:

■ Client interviews or meetings for follow-up are the occasions when you together with your client look in the rear-view mirror and also look forward. No one but the knowledge provider is able to lead this communication and ask the right questions, eg in a yearly development talk, an idea described in Chapter 5.

■ Client clubs for the exchange of experiences and contact possibilities. These clubs are usually of greater value to the clients than to yourself, but you can make them mutually valuable by inviting your clients to share your knowledge.

■ Letters in which you do not forget to wish your client all the best for the future. Tell the client about a new book, send a copy of an article, advise of useful contacts.

■ Knowledge letter, instead of a newsletter or a customer magazine. Knowledge very seldom has the character of a novelty but has a more long-term value. Customer magazines tend to focus more on the sender's own organization than the client's need for knowledge. A knowledge letter focused on this need is another way of keeping in touch with your clients and with the target groups in your contact network.

Between colleagues and teams

Internal communication about how to make knowledge grow, where to find the right knowledge and how to coordinate activities about goals and visions is a subject we will discuss further in Chapter 6. For now, here are some alternatives to improve internal communication:

■ Meeting policy—What goals do the different internal meetings have? Is there any time for reflection and analysis?

■ Internal mediation of news—Is there a need for mediation or is the need more for sharing and participating?

■ Informal ways of communication—Do you have any 'side-tracks' or short cuts to make the internal communication more efficient?

With suppliers

Since companies often forget their suppliers in their communication, why not ask yourself:

- Which of our suppliers should receive invitations to events we participate in or arrange?
- Which of our suppliers should receive more information about our knowledge area through, for example, our 'knowledge letter'?

Summary

Communication is the strategy for developing an optimal chain of activities. Professionals have access to many different communicative media for client education.

ASK YOURSELF AND YOUR TEAM MEMBERS:

- How do we involve key people and use key forums in order to arouse interest and give ideas to our target markets?
- What knowledge do we impart to our different target groups to help them to form an opinion of us, to choose us and to make the most accurate statements about us?
- How do we use ourselves as channels of communication and what media do we choose in order to create a demand, anchor ideas, involve our clients, and follow up our client relationships?

SUMMARIZING THE Cs

Summing up information on six of the seven Cs will enable you to decide and formulate your future demand and business development. A consistent approach, a clear goal and use of the six Cs will help you to see business possibilities for you/your company/organization as well as your markets. We would like to conclude this chapter by providing you with an illustration of how a knowledge company integrates all seven Cs in its projects as well as the entire company's development and attitude. The company in question is the JP (Jaakko Pöyry) Group. It has consistently built their business development, organization and marketing in line with the success factors for a knowledge-based company.

The **JP Group** was established in Helsinki, Finland, in 1958 and with 5000 employees worldwide is now the world's largest management-owned consulting and engineering firm within its market. It has specialized mainly in serving forestry, but also other process industries on a global basis through carrying out study and engineering projects. Its projects range from feasibility studies, conceptual design, basic and detail engineering to construction management, training of personnel and start-up assistance.

The JP Group has made its *choice of clients* and target markets through the choice of a very specific niche. In this niche it has identified the most important geographical key segments and on the basis of these it has located regional offices, served by several local offices. These offices have the responsibility for building confidence and establishing long-term relationships with clients in their geographical segment, in order to secure a long-term engagement in the market backed by the corporate know-how: local presence, global resources.

Through carrying out thousands of studies and engineering assignments within its niche (many of them for long-term 'repeat' clients) JP gets the opportunity of collecting valuable knowledge about its markets. This is a good example of *client information*, which it collects very systematically. It has also developed internal 'critic-meetings' as an internal source of information, and strategic 'critic-meetings' together with clients as an external source of information. It is a certified user of the quality system ISO 9001 which also helps the company to collect client information.

As an assignment involves a great deal of risk for the client, JP has developed its own conduct of knowledge responsibility and is carefully thinking through its clients' *chain of value*. It assists the client in picturing possibilities—product future, competitors, change and development in the product process, market possibilities, etc. To be able to give that picture, experience from JP's own track record is not enough. Therefore, it constantly scans and collects information from a variety of areas concerning the client niche, all over the world. Without a broad *contact network* this would be impossible.

All this information is kept in databanks, as a basis for further analysis from which the company is able to form future-oriented opinions. A misjudgement based on this data could be disastrous, not only for JP itself but for the whole market. Through this collected information, about clients as well as their markets, JP is able to adopt a global perspective on any investment plan or engineering problem.

It is able to encompass its clients' entire production chain from identification of project concept to marketing of the finished product. It sees trends and future client needs at a very early stage, which enables it to identify and develop new competence, methods, processes and craftsmanship to meet client demands effectively.

When continuously developing all this knowledge, and forming opinions based on collected data and statistics, the JP consultants are often invited to make speeches. They carefully select important seminars, conferences and congresses, at which consultants should be the key speakers. Events they have identified as important but are not invited to, they actively try to become involved in as they see these occasions as excellent opportunities for their *client education* and transferring of usable knowledge.

All employees are seen as JP sales people and everyone, even the managers, works in projects with clients, developing client relationships. The JP Group does not produce lots of corporate brochures or leaflets. Instead it has developed a *communication strategy* based on employees' personal contacts. As a communication and educational aid JP has developed:

- continuous 'multiclient studies', dealing with various aspects concerning clients on their whole market, such as capacity structure, market trends, prices, technological developments, financial developments, financial performance, cost competitiveness;
- the initiating of reports. When JP identifies a certain need for information it contacts the client concerned. If interested in the information, the client participates in and shares costs for working out a report or a study on the subject;
- tailormade reports to individual clients based on the data from its databank.

The JP Group has developed its own code of conduct and its own 'culture' based on shared attitudes. It has worked out an employment strategy as a part of its *competence strategy*, and does not, for example, employ students, only experienced consultants. It works with internal sponsorship and consultant rotation between regional offices. The JP Group management meets regularly to discuss technical and economic issues to ensure effective use of JP Group's resources. Project teams are formed with participants from different countries and different regions.

References

Christopher, Martin, Adrian Payne and David Ballantyne (1991) *Relationship Marketing*, Butterworth-Heinemann, Oxford.

Christopher, Martin, Adrian Payne and David Ballantyne (1993) 'Relationship investing', *Business Week*, March 15.

Forsyth, Patrick (1992) *Marketing Professional Services: A Handbook*, Pitman, London.

Graham, John R (1990) 'Customer education will be edge of new decade', *Marketing News*, May 28.

Höhler, Gertrude (1992) 'Mit den Augen des Kunden sehen', *Verkauf & Marketing Kommunikation*, No 6.

MacErlean, Neasa (1993), 'What's in a name?', *Professional Marketing*, Practice Profile, May.

Petersen, Frank af and Johan Bjurström (1991) 'Identifying and analyzing 'intangible assets'', *Journal of European Mergers and Acquisitions*, M&A Europe, September–October.

Zeithaml, V A (1981) 'How customer evaluating processes differ between goods and services', in James H Donnely and William George (eds), *Marketing of Services*, Chicago, American Marketing Association.

5

Client Relationship Management

'Communication is to relationships what breathing is to maintaining life.'

Virginia Satir

This chapter concentrates on the professional's activities and behaviour during the process of creating and maintaining client relationships.

'Those employees who deal directly with customers day after day have a powerful effect on customer loyalty,' says Frederick Reichheld. 'Long-term employees can serve customers better than newcomers can; after all, a customer's contact with a company is through employees, not the top executives. It is with the employees that the customer builds a bond of trust and expectations, and when those people leave, the bond is broken.'

To facilitate knowledge professionals' management of long-term client relationships, reference is made here to the four phases presented in Chapter 2. Since the aim of knowledge professionals is to fulfil their clients' expectations in terms of results, changes and improvements, none of the four phases in Figure 5.1 can be excluded from the concept of marketing knowledge. Client relationships are *your* responsibility.

While proceeding through these phases during the course of this chapter, our approach will concentrate on how to relate them to a behavioural framework. This perspective is radically different to traditional marketing techniques aimed at attracting clients through mass communication, advertising and direct marketing and sales. Such techniques were, and often still are, to help sales people 'close' their deals. If they promise the earth and do not live up to expecta-

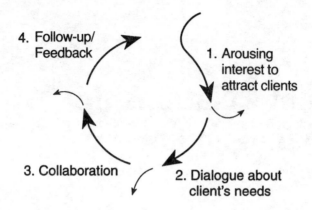

Figure 5.1   The four phases of the client relationship

tions, then who cares? There are so many other new prospects out there to hunt!

For knowledge and knowledge-intensive products, however, the idea of 'closing' hardly seems appropriate. This attitude needs to be entirely inverted so that people start thinking in terms of *opening*. Both parties—professional and client—are going to enter into, ie start, a mutually developing relationship. In knowledge businesses, it is in the collaboration phase that the real marketing takes place. The knowledge 'sales person' does not leave the scene. During this phase, the true marketer's role comes into focus—that of being a knowledge creator, business partner, supporter, teacher. If the knowledge professional/marketer does this well, the client will duly become a contributer and recommender. To assure results and quality it is of the utmost importance mutually to identify, express and agree on the goals. This is the basis for later evaluation of the results of collaboration.

ENDING ONE ASSIGNMENT HERALDS THE START OF THE NEXT

An often overlooked phase in marketing is the fourth, follow-up phase. The following story illustrates what happened to a group of consultants when, thanks to a crisis, they discovered the dynamics of client relationship management.

A prestigious consultancy became the subject of an image-analysis survey that had interviewed major buyers of consultancy services. According to the survey (presented in an exclusive business journal), the company was not ranked as a winner. This information shocked the managers who had always thought their company was the most sought-after consultancy in their field. They decided to transform this incident into a new way of working with quality. Whereas before they had never followed up their assignments, they now implemented a follow-up meeting on completing a client project. Instead of meeting the project leader, the client would meet one of the project leader's colleagues. This was to avoid the possible consequences of a close client/project leader relationship which could inhibit the client making statements about any shortcomings or lack of results. The structure of such follow-up meetings was put down in the form of an interview guide and developed by the consultancy.

The majority of such meetings turned out to be much more than follow-up meetings. As a result, after only one year, the managers could identify three positive effects:

- positive feedback and credit that had not previously been communicated to them enabled them to reinforce the behaviour and working methods appreciated by the clients;
- constructive criticism helped them to work with quality improvement;
- a new dialogue about new needs took place. When the clients had the opportunity to discuss the past, they began thinking forward and started questioning themselves: How can our development proceed to meet the needs of tomorrow? What new actions have to be taken?

Before the consultants realized it, they found themselves in new dialogues about needs and the outcome was sales meetings where the client took the initiative.

As Frederick Reichheld asserts: 'Once a company has identified the customers it *should* keep, it has to go about the business of keeping them. Often that means adding new products and services to meet customers' evolving needs. Companies that fail to use their knowledge of customers to develop the product or service those people will need next are leaving the door open for another company to lure them away.'

In Chapters 2 and 3, we discussed how you can use six Cs to develop your business and to plan your marketing and client relationships. Making a summary of all your intentions in the planning process provides you with a means to gain greater insight into appropriate roles for different parties in a knowledge-based business relationship. The six Cs are practical guidelines for preparing communications with potential, current and previous clients.

We now need to address the four behavioural roles that knowledge professionals would benefit from by becoming familiar with their implications for managing and developing client relationships. These roles are shown in Figure 5.2. Briefly, they are:

- Inspirer;
- Facilitator;
- Colleague;
- Knowledge Enhancer.

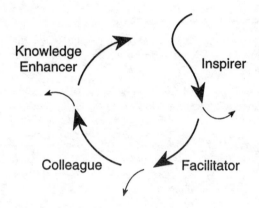

Figure 5.2   The professional's four key roles

BEHAVIOUR IN THE FIRST PHASE: YOU ARE AN INSPIRER

Your goal in this phase of the client relationship is to create an interest in your knowledge and confidence in your company so that the chosen clients take the initiative to contact you. Your aim here is to arouse the *right* kind of interest, to give your future clients the right ideas and insight into their needs, so that when they 'knock on your door', you are able to proceed effectively in your sales dialogue.

When sharing your knowledge, think of where to focus your 'knowledge spotlight'. What subjects, questions and situations should you illuminate and focus on in terms of your clients' worlds? The light should be on your clients and *their* business area, not on you, your skills, your company, its benefits, your work and its progress.

A group of healthcare specialists sent out invitations for a seminar on preventive healthcare. Talks and presentations were given by experts from the group as well as from hospitals and other organizations. However, they made a fatal mistake: every time a specialist from the healthcare group talked, a colleague would interrupt to promote the group.

This tactic totally 'backfired' since the participants questioned the professionalism and trustworthiness of the group. In retrospect, comments and subjective opinions on the group's skills should not have been made by the group themselves. Instead the participants themselves should have been left free to draw their own conclusions.

* * *

A computer company arranged a seminar and one of its consultants gave a 20-minute talk on the then novel subject of outsourcing. He started by recounting what his company had to offer, the advantages of its organization and other information about his company. Next he presented the company's idea of outsourcing and began to talk on the subject. Unfortunately, the participants started to query the company's experience and resources within the area and compared the company with its competitors. The atmosphere became awkward and embarrassing and, due to lack of time, the consultant was unable to correct the situation.

What he should have done instead was address the issue of outsourcing, its pros and cons, arouse the audience's enthusiasm and willingness to learn more or develop thoughts and ideas on the subject. When summarizing he should have mentioned that outsourcing was one of his company's new services.

Your clients decide how good you are

Subjective opinions, such as 'We are market leaders in . . .' or 'We provide the best . . .' are not to be put forward by you; they are conclusions your clients draw when listening to you, hearing about you, being in contact with you or working together with you.

Your task and responsibility are to highlight the benefits your clients will derive from your interest and concern, and from the knowledge you share with them.

An editor, who had targeted engineers and high-tech companies, felt unchallenged by his assignments and started planning a new presentation brochure about his skills. Instead of describing all his talents, he produced a leaflet with 27 short tips for engineers or technicians on how to write technical texts. He transferred knowledge that engineers and technicians needed which resulted in the clients themselves doing minor projects. The editor was contacted to work on more challenging projects and to produce more difficult texts. He even arranged seminars on how to simplify difficult technical texts. In this way he also learned more himself. He wrote articles in professional journals for engineers and willingly let them share his knowledge. Today he is regarded as a top expert within the field. This he managed to do without boasting about himself. What he did was to impart knowledge and thereby gain credibility.

* * *

A consultant was invited to give a speech at a seminar for corporate leaders. He had shortly before written a comprehensive document on the subject of leadership and wondered whether he should distribute a copy of it to the participants. He decided he would, and it just so happened that a journalist was present at the seminar.

This journalist used the document as background information in an article he wrote for a business paper and referred to the consultant as if the article was in the form of an interview. As a result, several clients got in touch with the consultant. Sharing knowledge here resulted in a 'snowball' effect.

To conclude, if you work well in this phase you will make optimal use of your time and skills. For example, instead of making ten 'cold calls' to ten 'prospects' who keep you at arm's length, you could create 25 people's interest in you and your knowledge by, for example, giving a presentation at a conference. These people would come to view you as an expert and knowledge professional as opposed to a pure sales person. One or two of them will probably contact you immediately after your presentation and perhaps a few more will contact you later on when the timing is right for them.

BEHAVIOUR IN THE SECOND PHASE: YOU ARE A FACILITATOR

'Do not judge a person from the answers he gives—judge him from the questions he asks.'

Voltaire

Your goal in this phase, when addressing the individual client company, is to obtain a mutual understanding of your potential client's problems, of the best possible strategy, and of the client's *commitment* to cooperate with you. Looking at this goal from a behavioural perspective, attention is paid to your ability to carry out a face-to-face dialogue with the potential client's representatives.

Let us now presume that your potential client company trusts you. The invitation to have a dialogue has been issued after having listened to you at a conference or having read about you and your company. In other words, your potential client company has developed an insight that constitutes a platform for continued dialogue about the company's needs.

When preparing for the meetings, put yourself mentally in your client company's position and think about what you should do in that situation. Consider what possible chain reactions the problems could result in, if measures are not taken. When later presenting your potential client representatives with the 'right' questions, you reveal how well you have understood the situation and will therefore increase their trust in your expertise. Understanding comes from really listening to what they say and do not say—ie listening to what they really communicate.

The slogan 'the client is always right' does not apply to the knowledge professional. Why? Because being a professional means that you have to be convinced that you are working with the right problem—otherwise how can you help your client effectively? It is the professional's responsibility to ensure that the right questions are asked and to question the client's own diagnosis of the company's problems. Through asking, you gather information that will lead you and your client further. Asking the right questions, in fact, is far more difficult than telling your client how to proceed. Your questions make your clients analyse their problems and needs and evaluate them. If clients do not truly understand their needs, they will not be able to decide on the right actions to take, nor will they be prepared to contribute to any effect.

The way others act

Look for models, professionals who have this client dialogue process 'in their blood'. What do they do? What kind of questions do they ask? How do they lead their clients forward? Someone who has studied client dialogues in depth is Neil Rackham. As a result of extensive research in more than 30 countries he has developed a method called SPIN. This method concentrates on asking questions that lead the clients to an understanding about their needs.

Rackham stresses two important 'secrets'—to think like the clients and to know what types of questions to ask. There are four categories of questions:

- Situation questions (to establish background information);
- Problem questions (about the client's problems, difficulties);
- Implication questions (about the implications of the problems);
- Need-payoff questions (about the value of solving the problems).

This method consists of several steps that cannot be covered in just one meeting. If you run too fast, your clients will feel stressed and lose their sense of motivation.

Proposals are joint creations

Far too many professionals prepare their proposals and/or contracts at too early a stage in the dialogue with their clients. These proposals and contracts are mostly based on assumptions and have not been part of the client dialogue. 'Proposal and price don't sell, but "real selling" does', is the title of an article by Alan Test about selling, proposal and price experiences. He says, '"Real selling" has nothing to do with preparing and presenting proposals that will, hopefully, justify the stated price. Real selling involves creating a relationship with a prospect, determining what the prospect needs or wants, and obtaining the prospect's agreement on the course of action you will take and on the price the prospect will pay . . . A proposal and price should not begin the sales process. They are what the salesperson and the prospect agree to during the sales process.'

The quality of the relationship between the salesperson and the client has a considerable impact on the probability of continued interchange between the parties in the future. This conclusion has been made by Crosby, Evans and Cowles. The findings of their study suggest 'that future sales opportunities depend mostly on relationship quality (ie trust and satisfaction) . . . Relational selling behaviours such as cooperative intentions, mutual disclosure, and intensive follow-up contact generally produce a strong buyer-seller bond.'

It is during the dialogue about the client's needs that the health and future well-being of the long-term client relationship is established. The more professionals focus on long-term relationships, the more clients perceive quality.

Facilitate your client's decision-making process

Help your clients make wise decisions. Involve them by giving one or more alternative suggestions. Use your experience to describe the consequences of each alternative solution and the different kinds of results that the client company can obtain. If you withhold possible alternatives, you are indirectly making the decision for your client. Remember, it is your client's decision. Through giving alternatives, you also give evidence of your experience.

There are different kinds of possible assignments connected to a hierarchy of purposes and goals. Consequently, your responsibility is to work out in advance, together with your client, what is expected of each party. Different types of assignments imply different types of needs, agreements, feedback and evaluation.

Arthur N Turner points out that a mutual understanding of goals influences the outcome of an assignment. He has identified and described eight fundamental objectives of consulting.These objectives are in hierarchical order (ie beginning at 1 and moving upwards to 8):

1. Providing information to a client.
2. Solving a client's problems.
3. Making a diagnosis which may necessitate redefinition of the problem.
4. Making recommendations based on the diagnosis.
5. Assisting with implementation of recommended solutions.
6. Building a consensus and commitment around corrective action.
7. Facilitating client learning, that is, teaching clients how to resolve similar problems in the future.
8. Permanently improving organizational effectiveness.

According to Turner, moving up in the hierarchy to reach ongoing organizational effectiveness requires greater sophistication and skill on the part of consultants and in how they manage the consultant/client relationship.

BEHAVIOUR IN THE THIRD PHASE: YOU ARE A COLLEAGUE

Your goal for this phase is to create optimal results for the client company and to make the collaboration a satisfactory experience for the client. You have to really *involve* your client to achieve good quality in all assignments and this is a responsibility shared by both parties. It is absolutely crucial at this stage that a knowledge professional avoids taking over a project and turning an assignment into a solo performance. Remember, it takes two to tango.

During the 1980s it was very popular to offer clients 'turnkey' projects, which meant that clients were spared any involvement at all. However, this approach finally proved disastrous for a computer consulting company.

Through trying to make a complete package of their knowledge, they had overlooked the client/consultant relationship of seeing one another as colleagues. They concluded that involving the client in the whole delivery process was essential for the final result and the client's experience of quality.

Your clients have a right to expect that you value their knowledge, ability and experience. Your role as a colleague is to be continuously aware of the benefits of having your clients as co-drivers throughout every assignment. You share your responsibility with them. This is especially important when one person has assigned you, another has approved the assignment and you work together with a third person. The competence, responsibility and efforts of both you and your client are needed to reach the established goals and to obtain the desired result and profit. In order to achieve good quality, you have to be aware of the way you communicate and how you help your clients develop.

Your way of collaborating with your clients in assignments will influence their future view of the quality you gave them. The more they are involved in each project, the more they can perceive the different dimensions of the quality you provide.

The knowledge professional's profile

Clients' expectations regarding your personal capabilities and qualities are something you have to consider carefully in order to develop the right behaviour in your relationship with them. What knowledge, abilities and behavioural factors characterize a good professional—from the *buyer's* point of view?

We have identified 13 factors of professional quality that knowledge buyers give priority to. These factors concern the professional's personal capacity, attitude, character and competence. They are linked to clients' perception of professionalism. The list of 13 factors is as follows:

- Professional/specialist knowledge.
- Knowledge of client's situation.
- Accurate perception and empathy.
- Analytical skills.
- Results orientation.
- Creativity.
- Integrity and courage.
- Teaching skills.
- Self-reliance.
- Communication skills.
- Ability to cooperate.
- Social skills.
- Ethics and moral competence.

One way to progress in your role as a knowledge professional is to identify the factors that you believe are most important for *your* current clients.

> To ensure quality and profits, a computer consulting company appointed a quality controller with two main responsibilities. One is to go directly into ongoing projects and ensure that consultants and clients get along well together. If they do not, he finds another consultant in order to obtain the best possible rapport. He also checks that plans are followed up and that clients are content. When projects are completed, it is the quality controller's responsibility to look into their profitability. He also initiates the development of new methods. When assigning the quality controller, the company's management had identified integrity, courage and analytical skills as the three most important factors that determine a controller's professional competence.

Knowledge markets need to be grounded in certain common values—ie that professionals treat client information as confidential and that an advertising agency, for example, never takes on assignments from two competitors. Although most business and professional areas have worked out their own code of conduct based on certain ethical principles, they do not automatically follow a neatly printed list of rules. True professional conduct issues from an inner feeling for ethical values that you and your colleagues adhere to. This we refer to as having a moral competence—a pertinent factor for knowledge professionals whose motto is: 'Knowledge is power'.

BEHAVIOUR IN THE FOURTH PHASE: YOU ARE A KNOWLEDGE ENHANCER

Your goal for this phase is to create a mutual consciousness of the value you created together with your client and to encourage the client to remain in a mutually developing business relationship with you and to act as your ambassador. Your role is to enhance both your client's and your own knowledge. This role is threefold, and therefore you need to:

- follow up, get and give feedback and learn through joint reflection and evaluation together with your clients;
- enable and encourage your clients to proceed independently;
- acknowledge, remember and consider what you did together in order to learn from the long-term results. If you do this

consciously, you use your clients as inspirers and evaluators of your own professional development.

One consultant told us that, after every assignment, he asked his client three questions:

- What is the best we have done together?
- What could we have done in another way?
- If we could repeat our joint project, in what way would we alter it?

Feedback is essential for a knowledge professional's progress and development. Common sources of client feedback are personal face-to-face interviews, written questionnaires and telephone calls, often conducted by people other than the professionals themselves.

Knowledge professionals should, however, personally follow up their assignments themselves together with their clients, for example in a 'client development talk'. The importance of this follow-up involvement of professionals is twofold since it consists of:

- a 'mirror' to reflect just how their methods and professional qualities have been developed and need to be developed further;
- a communication tool to maintain client relationships and to direct the conversation to new client needs, which can then point towards future assignments.

In our experience, few clients regard follow-up and feedback as an imposition on their time. On the contrary, they mostly welcome and appreciate that someone takes an active and long-term interest in their situation.

Dick Weiss (referred to in Chapter 3), states: 'Clients want to know, almost want to feel, that their consultants consider them important. When asked to participate in a follow-up meeting, practically all clients are willing to do so. The best way to conduct the interview is by using a standard questionnaire, although in this case the questionnaire is not handed over to the client; it is used as a tool of reference for the professional. These evaluation meetings can be very successful, both in learning the client's point of view and in finding additional work for the same client.'

When preparing your 'client development talk' next time, consider the four dimensions shown in Figure 5.3 which look both to the past and the future.

Focus your questions in the order indicated in Figure 5.3. Start from the position of looking back at the results from your projects/knowledge. Then direct the discussion forward, towards the

Knowledge quality (results)

1.
results from your
knowledge/product

2.
future needs

**Collaboration
– past**

**Collaboration
– future**

3.
satisfaction

4.
expectations

Service quality

Figure 5.3 Client development talk

future development of the client company's organization and their needs. Summarize what you have heard and give some ideas as to how your knowledge could contribute to their development. Conclude by asking for your client's opinion of the service quality aspects of your collaboration and your company. What aspects of your service are most appreciated and what are the client company's expectations for your future collaboration?

Use a questionnaire

Here is a three-step framework to help you prepare your interview guide:

1. Client values, results

Focus on the goals set for the project. Ask:
- How well have the goals been reached?
- What further values have been created?
- What changes have been initiated? Refer to the three dimensions of values: intrinsic; extrinsic; financial (see Chapter 3).
- What has not been reached and why?
- What can both parties do and learn from this?

2. Development of client needs

This is the beginning of a new dialogue about new needs. Ask about:

- The clients' view of the development in their business area.
- Threats and opportunities facing the client company's business.
- Actions that need to be taken to face a new situation.
- Additional knowledge/support needed in order for them to proceed.

3. Collaboration and service quality

Focus on the client company's experience of your collaboration. Ask about:

- Their views on your company's service quality.
- Strengths and weaknesses in the collaboration.
- Methods you should develop to improve your service quality.

Remember to also give your own opinion on your clients' role in the collaboration.

A psychologist consultancy carried out fifty personal client preparatory interviews to introduce a service quality system. They decided to conduct the interviews themselves instead of leaving them to the consultants of a quality firm. While conducting the quality interviews they found themselves in the middle of a new dialogue about client needs. As a result of the survey, they got several new assignments. Today they give priority to certain clients and assignments and follow them up with a personal interview. This is not always done by the psychologist responsible for that client but by a colleague. It is not part of the quality project either but as a business development and sales activity.

Self-assessment

The knowledge company that wants to survive in a competitive business environment has to create tools, set up procedures and define responsibility for relationship management and quality assurance. This is as crucial for the small, independent consultancy as for the multinational giant knowledge organization.

Coopers & Lybrand, employing about 67,000 accountants, consultants and service employees worldwide, have recognized their need to enhance their approach to provide a consistent level of relevant, responsive and superior services to clients. As an assignment for an international corporation can involve around 150-300 professionals internationally on a yearly basis, the implementation of procedures for client focused quality development is crucial.

Through international partner cooperation,Coopers & Lybrand have formulated common policy statements—Coopers & Lybrand Client Service Approach. Implementation is carried out through training and development programmes and through an extensive internal guide as support. The Client Service Approach Implementation Guide is a handbook covering senior partner experiences, guidelines and models, such as how to establish the service team, formulate the service strategy, manage the client relationship, communicate within the team, involve the client and measure success.

One of the tools used by Coopers & Lybrand's professionals is a self-assessment form for performance assessment, created by one of their partners. 'I have found it helpful to assess performance on an ongoing basis. I use the one-page "self-assessment" form to focus on key issues. I don't report the results to anyone – I use the form as a "stabiliser": to make sure that we're responding to developments as we need to.'

The self-assessment form helps the professionals to grade the performance of the lead partner and the team in relation to a specific client. The performance grading, ranging from 1 to 5 covers, eg assessment of level of:

- activity (both lead partner's and the team's);
- business knowledge (client information);
- internal communication (eg regular team meetings);
- service strategy (eg documentary evidence of plans);
- client input (eg systematic input from client executives);
- acknowledgements of the client;
- service penetration;
- profitability and volume.

In a small consultancy, the creation of the tools can be a bottleneck, due to lack of time, competence and financial resources. In a large firm, with great resources for internal development, it is the implementation that is the challenge.

Individual client care

At this stage, knowledge professionals have to be really careful not to just drop and forget their clients whilst chasing after new and seemingly more exciting ones. If you want to collaborate with your client company in new assignments, you have to keep in touch with them, showing that you care for their business in the long term. Through your interest, your clients will also show interest and become your ambassadors and recommend you.

An internationally well-known management consultant markets himself solely through taking initiatives for his clients and other members of his network as regards development of their knowledge. When he reads a book he thinks would benefit some of his clients, he buys several copies. He sends them as presents with personal comments on why he thinks the book could be of value. He also copies articles from international media which he posts or faxes to those clients he considers to have need of the knowledge. This he calls Relationship Marketing and is the kind of marketing he once used in order to retain a client he collaborated with. He kept in touch showing his genuine interest for the client's personal development and business progress, and a willingness to make himself useful. After five years of thoughtful foresight, the client contacted him. The client company was in the middle of a huge reorganization and they wanted him during this process.

Business organizations change—relationships remain

Business World, an advertising agency in Frankfurt-am-Main, is a young up-and-coming company that has based its expansion on excellent management of close business relationships.

Business World's business idea is to offer knowledge, creativity and services to clients who sell knowledge, services and products to companies, organizations and professionals. Håkan Verner-Carlsson, one of the two founders, describes how two of their client relationships developed and how he learned that selling advertising services has little to do with advertising in a classical sense.

'When I worked as an executive director at the international agency, J Walter Thompson, in Frankfurt, one of our client companies was Frankfurter Allgemeine Zeitung. Our assignment was to create a demand for FAZ as an advertising medium and we appreciated the person we worked for—we appreciated his style and his product. We understood each other. And yet despite this, our client later changed to another agency, but I stayed in touch.

'A couple of years later, my future partner, Jochen Vollback, and I decided to make a reality of our dreams, to start an agency of our own. We chose to specialize in business-to-business advertising/marketing communications. When we had the basic outline of our business idea, we asked for feedback from people we respected and trusted. One of the people we asked included our former client at FAZ. Our question to him was simple, "How do you, as a buyer of advertising agency services, look upon our business idea?"

Our planned half-hour meeting extended into a three hour discussion of market conditions and client/agency relationships. We learned about the problems he experienced through the lack of continuity in personal relationships between client and agency when an agency changes people too frequently. Knowing the senior management was not enough. "We want competent and creative account directors who serve us on a continuous basis, who are involved in and understand our business". He liked our business idea and ended by saying, "Maybe we will work together some day in the future". Within a year of having started Business World he approached us and asked, "Would you be interested in taking part in a competitive presentation?"'

Verner-Carlsson described the development of another client relationship in the following way, 'In my former position as an executive director of JWT I hired a lot of young account directors and trainees. Among all the candidates I interviewed, there was one young man with whom I felt a strong mutual understanding, Patrik Bernstein. I hired Patrik and we developed a confidential mentor/mentee relationship. Patrik moved on to work in Asia but we kept in touch, sending each other information, calling now and then for advice, etc. Years later Patrik became Managing Director of a Unilever Company in Germany. He called me up on the phone and said that he was back in Germany and in need of an agency for corporate communications. Could we come and present our agency to his management group?..... '

This last example confirms just how important good relationships with former employees, colleagues and other 'investors' are—they too are ambassadors and could be potential clients.

Clients as partners

Why not establish a joint venture and develop something new together with your client? How about starting a project for developing a new system, a new method for calculation, a new programme of education? By combining your different competences, you could offer them in a joint venture to reach a common market.

Together with their client, two consultants had worked out a major programme for educating all employees. After successfully completing the project, the two consultants and client decided to develop and adapt the programme in partnership to suit other organizations in a similar situation. Through pooling their joint competences, knowledges and experiences, the programme has now begun to sell on a royalty basis to a wide range of knowledge-based companies and institutions.

Activate your client as your recommender by transferring more samples of knowledge to them. Send them a 'knowledge/newsletter', a personal letter, a fax, an interesting article. Or give them a 'bonus' by mediating an important personal contact. Do not turn your back on them, keep on showing interest in them and stay in touch.

You have invested a great deal of time, knowledge and care in your client relationships. This is a fortune you have created! See to it that you both manage and enhance this asset! Acquire more knowledge, prepare yourself for the next dialogue about needs. Do not let the circle turn into a merry-go-round without any new input. When a client relationship functions well, it provides a mutual source of business development.

ASK YOURSELF AND YOUR TEAM MEMBERS:

- How do we look upon sharing knowledge with our chosen markets, and to what extent should we share this knowledge before getting paid?
- What measures do we take in order to facilitate our potential clients in their decision-making process?
- What is the personal quality profile of a knowledge professional in our organization?
- What measures do we take in order to enhance the knowledge that both we and our clients have acquired as a result of mutual experiences?

References

Crosby, Lawrence A, Kenneth R Evans and Deborah Cowles (1990) 'Relationship Quality in Services Selling: An Interpersonal Perspective', *Journal of Marketing*, Vol 54.

Rackham, Neil (1987) *Making Major Sales*, Gower Publishing Company Ltd, Hampshire.

Reichheld, Frederick F (1993) 'Loyalty-based Management', *Harvard Business Review*, March–April.

Test, Alan (1992) 'Proposals and price don't sell, but "real selling" does', *Marketing News*, Vol 26, no 7.

Turner, Arthur N (1982) 'Consulting is more than giving advice', *Harvard Business Review*, September–October.

6

Invest in Future Business Opportunities

'The rate at which individuals and organizations learn may become the only sustainable competitive advantage, especially in knowledge-intensive industries.'
Chairman and President, Analog Devices

The knowledge company has two major intangible assets—its client capital and its competence capital. This chapter deals with how to develop competence. We look at how your company/unit organizes its learning processes for business development and the future harvesting of knowledge.

SYSTEMIZE YOUR LEARNING PROCESSES

Competence is *the* attraction factor for knowledge companies. It acts like a magnet and as such is your most competitive tool to attract both clients and outstanding professionals. Just take a few minutes to think about what motivates your highly successful colleagues. Is it primarily wealth that drives them? Or do they value other factors such as challenging assignments and learning from other top-notch professionals?

A parallel can be drawn between knowledge companies' investment in competence development and industrial companies' investment in research and product development. However, whereas R&D has traditionally been in the hands of a select few, knowledge-intensive companies have to learn how to *integrate* learning processes into all their client projects and marketing activities. This process involves everyone in a knowledge company and each individual needs to keep a constant focus on developing competence and managing both client relationships *and* colleague relationships.

Continual competence development tends to be elusive and difficult to put into practice on a conscious, regular basis. People talk about teaming their core abilitites and yet little is done to systemize them in practical terms.

HOW CAN YOU CAPTURE COMPETENCE?

There seem to be six main bottlenecks when it comes to seizing competence effectively in knowledge-based businesses. The major one is not capital so much as *time*. Knowledge professionals such as engineers, doctors, scientists and lawyers already work long hours, so asking them to do more could be a delicate issue. Another block for professionals is to accept their *responsibility* in terms of learning and teaching—ie to assist others apart from just themselves. Thirdly, many professionals experience *difficulty in teaching* others about their knowledge. Furthermore, many professionals tend to be *defensive* in terms of prestige and knowledge and are often more loyal towards themselves and their professions than their companies.

Two more bottlenecks are *organization* and *communication*. Results depend on how work is organized and an 'eagle perspective' is needed to avoid divisions/units/individuals going off in different directions. With numerous kinds of specialist knowledge, professionals are increasingly representing varied languages and cultures which puts a premium on effective communication skills.

Helping professionals change the way they learn is a powerful and compelling means to develop their competence on an ongoing basis. Therefore, this chapter focuses on how professionals and leaders of knowledge companies can leverage their time to ensure that the processes of creating client value are integrated with the responsibilities of internal communication, learning and teaching. Knowledge leaders, in particular, need to ask critical questions at regular intervals about their established processes and ways of working. Leaders have to be able to develop new definitions and concepts and to balance differences of opinion and possible conflicts so that insecurity and the need for new competences are both dealt with successfully. With such a conscious approach firmly embedded in a knowledge company, its professionals can proactively contribute to business development, survival and prosperity.

When people first start their careers at the pharmaceuticals company **Hoffman La Roche** in Basel, Switzerland, emphasis is placed on developing their professional skills—ie their tools to do a job.

The divisional human resources strategy at Hoffman La Roche is to support professionals to learn through their everyday experience by enlarging the context of their jobs and providing them with regular professional training. During the next stage of a professional's career, focus is put on developing human skills. Importance is placed on the individual's ability to achieve results with and through other people. At Hoffman La Roche these skills are mainly developed through coaching, performance management, job rotation and project management.

During the third stage of development conceptual skills are stressed—the ability to understand and relate to complex issues. The chief ways of developing conceptual skills, according to Hoffman La Roche, are demanding new assignments and international assignments. Support is mainly in the form of a wide selection of information, educational training and meetings. Furthermore, everyone at Hoffman La Roche has the right to change jobs if, after five years, professionals no longer feel their current positions are providing them with opportunities for optimal learning.

SEVENTH C: COMPETENCE DEVELOPMENT

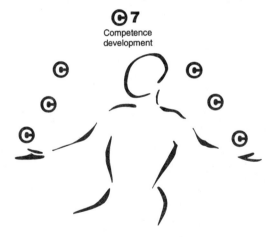

C7
Competence
development

Since competence is your prime magnet, we have analysed the concept in more detail to isolate the components knowledge companies need to focus on. Through working, studying and exchanging views with a broad cross-section of truly competent knowledge professionals throughout the world, our research suggests that competence comprises an *integration* of the following criteria:

Knowledge	concepts, facts, methods, a 'system' of information
Experience	accumulation of knowledge, insights
Integrity	values, self-knowledge, congruence
Innovation	creativity to apply ideas to productive use and to sytematically challenge the status quo
Communication	contacts, networks, relationships, possibilities and influence in different national and corporate cultures
Motivation	assertiveness and determination to achieve results
Flexibility	ability to change behaviour and thinking processes to match the prevailing circumstances

The above seven criteria sketch a generalized 'picture' of competence. Leaders of specific projects, assignments, departments, etc will have to define their own competence profiles.

Direct and manage your competence

To produce knowledge effectively in today's global, market-driven environment, leaders and professionals in knowledge companies have an essential role to play in creating and managing a dynamic system of interaction. Individuals in traditional hierarchical organizations have fixed positions, as in a symphony orchestra. In contrast, knowledge professionals interact, as in a jazz band. For jazz musicians the music is not a finished score, the key lies in each individual's competence to play jazz and to improvise to make new music. They depend on one another and the 'audience'/clients to develop their performance as a continuous process of making new connections and new possibilities.

The role of knowledge leaders is twofold. One is to find ways of putting different types of jazz bands together so that a new synthesis of knowledge can be made. A second aspect is to find an appropriate balance between:

■ the flexibility and informality needed for innovative thinking; and
■ the systems and processes required when a business grows and becomes more complex.

A further element is needed—for knowledge leaders to identify their 'star' performers and to help them to understand both the ingredients of their success and how they can describe their 'recipe' to others.

Symbols and metaphors

Understanding calls for an elegant command of language so that leaders and professionals can clearly explain what type of expertise they have. Through using language that is simple and yet profound, professionals can help create a dynamic culture of learning that influences one another's behaviour and action in positive ways.

Eckhart Wintzen, president and chief executive of BSO/Origin, an international information technology company with its headquarters in Utrecht, Holland, has described his way of using clear language and dynamic thinking (in Geary, 1993). When asked to explain the origins of his company, Wintzen says, 'When I started out, I was fortunate in that I was not hindered by any knowledge of proper management techniques. Otherwise, I might have ended up doing things the traditional way.' He also applies the 'cell-division' philosophy of corporate organization and illustrates his approach in biological terms: 'In nature, things grow without any supervision. An onion, for example, grows because it has a message built into its cells, not because it has a chairman of the board. And if nature can do it, why can't companies?'

Translated into everyday language, the cell-division approach means that when a branch of BSO/Origin has a staff of more than 100, it divides into two. This keeps the company commercially flexible and as Wintzen says, 'Our employees love the cell-philosophy approach, because it allows them maximum play for their own initiative and creativity. By keeping staff limited to 100, people are really able to see the fruits of their own labour.' BSO/Origin consists of 80 'cells' operating in 14 countries in the Far East, North and South America and Europe.

Let us now take a closer look at the type of corporate climate that fosters competence that:

- identifies and satisfies client needs profitably on a long-term basis;
- fulfils professional needs within the organization.

Climate and culture

> *'Our business is really 80 per cent communication and 20 per cent computing.'*
>
> Eckhart Wintzen

What characterizes the culture of excellent knowledge companies? To begin with, the people working in such organizations are peers and colleagues, rather than bosses and subordinates. Leaders obtain their power through the consensus of their colleagues. Natural leaders and 'knowledge executives' grow through their professional excellence and ability to market their ideas internally. The two major challenges for leaders are to lead professionals in their management of both business development and learning.

To profit from all the hours spent communicating with clients, colleagues, networking partners, competitors, etc, knowledge professionals have to know how to integrate learning into their everyday activities and projects. They need practical tools that enable them to identify special areas of new knowledge more quickly than competitors and to share them effectively throughout the organization.

Such learning processes require trust and open channels of communication. This puts pressure on knowledge leaders to be models of highly effective communication in their daily meetings with colleagues. Their role is to foster a climate in which generous dialogue thrives.

Daily Drama Ltd is a corporate training institute that specializes in the psycho-social working environment of professionals such as leaders, doctors and managers. Daily Drama is run by psychologist, actress and author Catharina Nasenius who maintains that effective organizations in the future have to have a culture that balances 'feeling' qualities such as sensitivity, care, flexibility and improvisation and 'rational' qualities such as large-scale plans, efficiency, facts, specialization and structure.

As knowledge companies are steered by ideas, leaders need to be fluent in creating forums for dialogue. To help leaders get to grips with the mechanisms of such dialogues and meetings, the actors at Daily Drama present leaders with typical issues they have to be able to deal with. Through a dramatic presentation of a real-life situation with set characters and script, the problem is laid bare. The actors then start a dialogue with their clients asking for advice on how to solve the problems depicted. Through such means, knowledge leaders are helped both to spot their mistakes *and* to internalize their learning of leadership skills.

COMPETENCE CULTURE

An effective culture for competence development within knowledge companies comprises the following eight criteria (see Figure 6.1). They are all interrelated and move the culture forward in terms of learning, insight and results:

1. Shared vision and knowledge goals.
2. Courage to take on demanding assignments.

3. Professionals responsible for their own learning—and that of others.
4. Focus on learning, tolerance and teaching.
5. Generosity in sharing knowledge with colleagues within the organization.
6. Openness to learning from mistakes and feedback.
7. Commitment to development through working via strategic partnerships and networks.
8. Clear concepts and methods for 'production' and quality assurance.

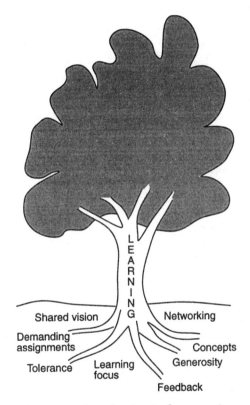

Figure 6.1   Eight interrelated criteria for creating an effective competence culture

Competence Culture 1: Shared vision and knowledge goals

'People support what they help to create.'

In knowledge companies, authority is founded on consensus. The type of leaders essential for knowledge companies are those who help professionals understand and see the underlying patterns of situations.

Consensus is also the foundation for solving conflict since leaders can help move people away from a conflict zone by pointing in a new direction which benefits everyone.

A shared vision is the basis for a selective learning strategy since it gives a structure for different groups in an organization to participate in and build ideas on. It acts both as a dynamo of corporate purpose and as a reminder—are we on course and are we developing the competence needed when we reach the destination?

When a shared corporate vision is matched and linked to individual knowledge goals, professionals become even more motivated since they acquire a mission that is rooted in the identity of their company and themselves as individuals. Once a knowledge company's identity and mission are in tune with its actions, the company becomes unstoppable. How could you prevent professionals from carrying out their goals if these are a natural expression of who they are?

Looking back to where we started in Chapter 3, every 'pilot' needs a map and compass to be able to reach the set goal. An effective shared vision includes both feelings and structure so that it sets the tone for an ongoing dialogue about present and future business ideas and knowledge goals. The vision of a knowledge company can be expressed through defining your preferred client categories and the values you are going to create for them. Your vision also contains a 'self-image' of your organization's competences and values.

When creating a shared vision, it is essential to step back from day-to-day activities. In this way, knowledge professionals can obtain a clearer picture of their clients' needs and their future business goals. However, since vision is not a question of thinking just about business results, people also need to get into another frame of mind. Such thinking cannot be forced and given specific deadlines, since it entails a balance between and 'interweaving' of conscious and unconscious thoughts.

The shared vision of all professionals is the core for creating clearly stated knowledge goals. Such goals help professionals to be selective in terms of their learning. A knowledge goal could, for example, comprise the following three points:

■ What is our core competence related to our present market and competitors?
■ What knowledge will our chosen clients need to enable them to meet their clients' future needs?

■ What knowledge do we need to develop within the next five years?

Adtec, an environmental company operating in Sweden, the UK and France, runs a 'WINGS' programme (Working In New Goal Setting). This programme relates to the company's external and internal total quality development. As a role model for the organization, Adtec has chosen the seagull from the book *Jonathan Livingstone Seagull* by Richard Bach. This book describes an individual who, through practice and training, constantly improves and sets new goals. The seagull, therefore, is a symbol for all quality improvement activities at Adtec.

Each employee selects his or her own knowledge goals based on the expectations of internal and external clients. Two hours of individual study are allotted every week.

The knowledge goals have to be measurable and have a time limit. Each person is to acquire role models or 'bentors' (benchmarking/mentors) both within and outside the company. Every Monday morning, the employees briefly review their learning projects and state which two hours during the coming week are to be spent on the programme.

At Adtec, these two hours are 'sacred' and all employees attain three to four knowledge goals during the course of a year.

The most critical responsibility of knowledge leaders in terms of knowledge goals is to provide clear expectations of performance and to outline those learning processes that add value to the company. Furthermore, leaders have to ensure that knowledge professionals receive regular feedback to keep in line with their goals. Finally, it is the knowledge leaders' responsibility to identify both examples of practical changes in behaviour and sources of changes.

Competence Culture 2: Courage to take on demanding assignments

'Nothing ventured—nothing gained.'

Since demanding assignments are the major source of inspiration, development and recognition for truly competent professionals, leaders of knowledge companies need to monitor this type of assignment carefully. The learning from such assignments needs to be systemized to benefit everyone in the organization, since most people learn most when they are forced to go beyond their own limits.

There have to be means for every professional to have the chance to take on assignments that give them the opportunity to solve 'new' problems and to try new ways of working.

Have you ever committed yourself to do an assignment which lay beyond your immediate scope of experience? Did you learn from the challenge? Figure 6.2 provides a model to illustrate different zones of challenge and learning that professionals in knowledge companies need to feel comfortable with.

The three zones of challenge and learning

Your role as a professional is to make your learning dynamic and to move between different zones of security and risk. It is a question of your being able to balance the joy of discovering/rediscovering, the sense of achievement through carrying out challenging assignments with the ability to withdraw for times of reflection. The responsibility of the leader and management is to support those professionals about to enter the outer zone of risk and to encourage those who need to experience these realms in order to develop. At times, a leader perhaps needs to intervene to help a professional pull back from extended moments of stress and accept a period of 'rest'.

1. *Comfort zone*. We all need this inner area of retreat from time to time in order to recuperate from any potential 'burnout' from never-ending streams of new projects and clients. This zone is comforting since it provides routines and well-known tasks in a familiar environment. The danger of too much security, however, is that we can go on doing the same old thing and not pay any attention to changing circumstances.
2. *Learning zone*. The middle zone should be familiar territory. Here, professionals have to learn something new and adapt them-selves in order to carry out assignments well. Working in a knowledge company means that you have to be in this zone most of the time. However, in order to prepare for and create your future, you also have to go out into a third zone.
3. *Challenge zone*. This is the area where you have to do something you have not done before or in a new way, or work together with professionals from new fields with whom you have never worked before. When you really put yourself in a challenging and perhaps risky learning process, you acquire the means of obtaining essential growth. As a knowledge professional, you have to be willing to enter risk zones which also means having to do things for the first time and risking mistakes. In highly competitive areas such as management consultancy, future business opportunities lie in that which is new—ie that which is risky.

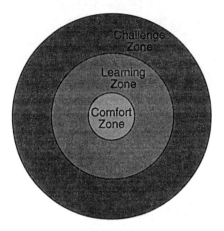

Figure 6.2   The three zones of challenge and learning

An important activity for knowledge companies is to find those key people who not only carry out demanding assignments but can also reflect and draw important conclusions from them. The cornerstone of such reflections is to understand the process of learning. Challenging assignments mostly give professionals opportunities for working with a wide variety of teams and groups plus the capacity to build on, process and improve other people's ideas.

This is just what McKinsey does in its Organization Performance Practice, OPP. Tom Peters outlines McKinsey's OPP structure in his book *Liberation Management*. The purpose of OPP is simply to take advantage of the knowledge that is built up in assignments and to feed that back to the professionals. This has been done through the creation of electronic databases and networks by a key manager, who in 1991 had the title 'director of knowledge management'. The firm also has a system called the Firm Practice Information System which consists of reports on lessons learned by project leaders on particular consulting assignments. Another is the Practice Development Network, a database of core documents contributed by each of the 31 practice centres.

The importance of teamwork

One source of competence development within professional organizations is for group members to become skilled in moving the work forward in terms of content and process. Whereas content describes *what* is done, process describes *how* something is done.

With process, group members need to be aware of various stages.

Each stage is part of a journey, and sometimes the going gets tough. It is a question of seeing this rough patch as a period of transition to the next stage. In this way, the members of a group can constructively help one another to negotiate obstacles and avoid the risk of getting stuck.

Jon Katzenbach and Douglas Smith emphasize the importance of groups as the main channel of corporate learning in the future. They classify projects into four groups:

- working group;
- pseudo-team;
- real team;
- high-performance team.

According to Katzenbach and Douglas, only when a group has worked through difficult issues and conflicts does it become a real group with the potential for high performance. Their research also confirmed that one of the conditions needed to help groups become high-performing teams is the presence of challenges and demands for results.

Competence Culture 3: Professionals are responsible for their own learning—and that of others

> 'The job of management in the knowledge-based organization is not to make everybody a boss. The task is to make everyone a contributor.'
>
> Peter Drucker

Here are three commandments for knowledge-based businesses:

- Knowledge professionals must be motivated to be life-long learners.
- All individuals are responsible for both their own learning and for teaching others.
- Everyone is responsible for creating new applications of their knowledge to new areas and thereby making knowledge productive and an asset for the organization.

Successful professionals therefore both understand the importance of the organization's continual learning and know they are responsible for this process. For example, they are responsible for marketing their ideas within the company so that they get the right resources to develop their ideas and to become involved in the project they want.

They learn how to ask pragmatic questions like: Is it useful? Is it practicable? Is it commercial?

To practice and develop such thinking, one international consulting company we carry out assignments for has the policy of having monthly presentations of new concepts and/or projects.

As two or three presentations are given simultaneously, and as attendance is voluntary, there is an inbuilt element of responsibility for each professional to communicate the value of his or her presentation beforehand to ensure people turn up to listen. Thus this company's consultants acquire ongoing practice in carrying out intensive knowledge 'marketing' campaigns among their colleagues.

A 'value-added' feature of these internal learning/teaching seminars is that knowledge professionals become better equipped to learn the language and purpose of marketing. They learn how to 'sell' their ideas in terms of the benefits provided to the listener/user, irrespective of whether the user is a client within the organization or outside. By having such thinking embedded in everyone's minds, the whole process of communicating with the market is trained on an internal 'market'. Turnaround becomes faster and totally market oriented.

With constant practice and feedback, everyone learns the importance of achieving results through working with others and by contributing towards others' competence. In such a win–win culture, everyone benefits since the focus is on creating client value and profitability for your own organization rather than on a few professionals hogging the limelight all the time. If your ultimate goal is to be famous for your knowledge, the best way for you to reach this step is to first help others to benefit from your knowledge, since they will then know what to recommend you for.

So the emphasis in knowledge-intensive organizations is on being able to learn, teach, produce and transfer knowledge and to conceptualize new knowledge. With this understanding firmly anchored, each professional can contribute towards achieving results-oriented learning. There are three steps to this strategy:

- See the large, macro picture—study the overall map of where you want to 'go' and what knowledge you will need to get there (vision).
- Have a clear, micro focus—isolate/zoom in to specific areas of learning on your map (knowledge goal).
- Make a detailed plan—work out how to learn this area of knowledge and how to transfer it to the rest of the organization (learning and teaching method).

The last step contains one of the keys to adding value, innovating and developing individual and organizational competence on a continual basis.

Competence Culture 4: Focus on teaching, tolerance and learning processes

> *'The range of what we think and do is limited by what we fail to notice.'*
>
> R D Laing

When knowledge companies highlight the central importance of learning, professionals have a means for looking to the good of the whole group/unit/organization instead of anxiously guarding their own reservoir of knowledge and prestige.

The whole process of learning can be conceived of in terms of three steps. The first one is *cognitive* in which new ideas are perceived. The next stage is more *behavioural,* when the implications of new ideas are internalized, and the third stage is when changes in behaviour result in *performance*, business development and quality improvements. Through highlighting the importance and dynamics of learning in knowledge companies, a whole range of opportunities emerge, as illustrated by the following two cases.

Once a month, the project leaders of an advertising agency met to gather information. These meetings were for 'mutual admirers'. Everyone was 'driven' to show how clever they were and how their colleagues succeeded in completing their latest project. Of course, their clients were incredibly pleased too . . .

Not once did anyone reflect on what they had learned and why their projects had succeeded so well. No one thought of asking, 'What was the reason for our fantastic success? What could we have done in a different way?' Not one single word was mentioned about 'failing'. The professionals at this advertising agency did not even want to express the word 'mistake' and therefore had no framework within which they could learn from them—let alone share their insights with others.

* * *

A hospital in Bern, Switzerland, has been very active in its teaching programmes to enhance the overall learning within the hospital. One of the main approaches is to help raise nurses' sense of self-esteem and to educate doctors to see the effects their 'star' status behaviour has on the hospital staff and patients.

Tolerance and learning processes are everyone's responsibility in knowledge-based organizations. Professionals need to be reminded constantly that they are working towards enlarging and empowering the scope of competence within their company/unit/division. When people's eyes, ears and feelings are focused on the importance of enhancing learning skills, they can start stepping over their fences of demarcation and defensiveness and move gently towards their colleagues.

When a group of professionals gets to grips with the process of learning, they can make huge improvements in their ability to communicate the benefits of their knowledge. Think back to your most recent presentations of your department/company and/or concept. Have you considered how you could help your audience understand more of your message through addressing different people's ways of listening and learning? Have you reflected too how such understanding can be one step further towards being able to accept individual differences?

To give another example, some people need to have very detailed, logical information before they can proceed in their learning, whereas detailed information can totally block others. All knowledge providers need to be aware of such distinctions.

One group that clearly knows how to benefit from such differences of learning to develop their knowledge is a highly qualified group of international inventors we have regular contact with.

They work according to a clearly defined learning process to develop their ideas which they then sell to companies. What happens is that company X approaches them and says they would like ideas on subject Y. The inventors then meet four times to isolate the most valuable ideas from which the client company is free to choose. During the first brainstorming meeting, a totally free rein is given to *all* ideas the group associates with. There is one rule and that is not to pass one word of judgement or criticism on any suggestion at this stage. During the second and subsequent meetings, a highly detailed approach is started in which a selective number of ideas are screened and subjected to analytical and logical thinking processes.

Our way of thinking 'programmes' our behaviour in a variety of set ways that can limit us unless we learn how to intervene and make changes. This is not to say that there is any correct way, or that any particular way of thinking is wrong. It is simply a matter of learning to become more flexible and open to new opportunities for learning in ways we had previously overlooked. Through learning how to learn and teach, we learn to increase our choices and make new 'pathways' in our brains. By practising and carrying out new behaviours, we develop our competence to help both ourselves and others to bring

successful strategies into conscious awareness. As a result, knowledge providers can increase the context of their knowledge and the
scope of their future business.

The more flexible and confident professionals become in their
learning and interaction with others, the less inclined they feel, for
example, to hide behind an 'expert' mask. Instead they can learn to
look at their clients and colleagues and ask themselves, 'How can I
learn from them?' or 'How can my colleagues help me to help them
understand the benefits of my knowledge?'

Competence Culture 5: Sharing knowledge with colleagues—as opposed to competing with them

> *'Knowledge is one of the few assets that you can give away
> and yet still retain.'*

Many people are blocked in their learning and teaching of others. This
occurs every time a specialist is 'stingy' in imparting knowledge in
order to guarantee future assignments and income. However, if
professionals reversed such a tendency to 'hoard' knowledge and
instead gave it away, they would most probably be assured greater
success.

We all have numerous opportunities for being generous with our knowledge to
help both others and ourselves. **Richard** and **Karen Holding** have a well-reputed
practice based in London. Richard, an osteopath by training, treats numerous
patients and also provides regular training for other osteopaths, chiropractors,
doctors and dentists throughout Europe and the USA. Karen, a lawyer and NLP
(Neurolinguistic Programming) Master Practitioner is currently in the process of
writing a handbook on NLP to enable individuals to learn for themselves how they
can practise and perfect powerful communication strategies. Richard's training
courses and Karen's book provide effective forums for structuring and sharing their
knowledge with both clients/partners/colleagues and 'competitors'.

Through being generous with knowledge and responsible for their
own learning and for teaching colleagues and clients, professionals
can receive new knowledge, strengthen their position as specialists in
their fields and thereby be assured of new assignments. Professionals'
fear of losing prestige and impact through sharing information and
knowledge with colleagues is a serious hindrance in numerous
knowledge-intensive companies.

One company that is making strident moves to overcome the negative consequences of this fear is engineering group ABB. With some 34,000 employees throughout the world, ABB has a vested interest in communicating to professionals the importance of not inventing the wheel twice. In an article in ABB Info Systems' newsletter Inforama (Olofsson, 1993), Hans Grunditz, ABB Power Generation, says that today many managers, construction engineers and companies withhold information that others need. They do this because they are terrified of losing prestige and influence as a result of sharing their information with other people. From a holistic perspective in terms of a company's knowledge and resources and the client's interest, such a situation is extremely wasteful.

Hans Grunditz also points out that ABB Power Generation has now introduced a Lotus Notes data-based information system which compiles client complaints, information on strategic planning, client focus projects, budgets and development projects. As a result, when project team members in Germany go home in the evening, they put their information into a database which is then opened by colleagues in the USA when they start work the next morning. They in their turn share their information in the evening with their colleagues in Japan, Australia and Europe. It is also possible to open up parts of this system of information for clients.

However, to be able to share your knowledge with colleagues, you need to know how to communicate it effectively. This sounds easier than it is in practice and three essentials are required to ensure that:

- we know what we say we know—if we are not firmly rooted in our knowledge, who will want to come back for more and who will recommend us to clients?
- we know what our colleagues need to know—this demands an ability on our part to put ourselves in colleagues' shoes. We also need to be informed about the projects they run, their clients and assignments;
- we know how to communicate/package knowledge to enable colleagues/team members to learn—in other words, we need to be good 'teachers/facilitators' and to be talented at making the 'invisible' visible.

One way of developing important insights about how to give and receive valuable knowledge is through engaging in 'quality' conversations. In the time-pressed world of professionals, how can such conversations be encouraged to occur on a regular basis? Frank

Becker, a professor at Cornell University, points out that 'companies need to devote more office space to creating places like well-tended living rooms, where employees can sit around and "chat".' Frank Becker calls himself an 'organizational ecologist' and is leading a two-year study on offices, financed by firms in America, Japan, Britain and Holland. Productive conversations enable professionals to create both key relationships and connections to other subject areas. The value of such conversations are the intangibles/'seeds' of knowledge that are left in the minds of those participating in the conversation.

Competence Culture 6: Openness for learning from mistakes and constructive feedback

> 'Experience is not what happens to you, it is what you do with what happens to you.'
>
> Aldous Huxley

Trial and error is a recognized method for developing new knowledge and skills. Nevertheless, we seldom have the opportunity to learn from other people's mistakes so that we can avoid typical professional hazards. Project accounting systems of consultancy companies are often state-of-the art descriptions in which colleagues learn of successes but little, or nothing, of obstacles and mistakes. In a culture which is dedicated to competence development, sharing difficulties and mistakes is encouraged so that new ways of learning can be explored together. A climate of cooperation and trust is also fostered.

Susan Ernst-Peters of Design for Business in Zurich, Switzerland, says, 'Whenever possible, after projects we set up a de-briefing/review (usually combined with a meal because this saves time and helps build the right atmosphere) with team members where each person has an opportunity to give feedback and share ideas to help us learn for the next project.' Dr Charles Savage of Digital maintains, 'Our research shows distrust adds 20 to 30 per cent to costs and causes a company to miss from 20 to 50 per cent of the opportunities staring it in the face.' In knowledge companies, *trust* is crucial. Its counterpart, *distrust,* is deadly and no knowledge-based business can afford the consequences of such a negative spiral.

Thomas Watson Sr, IBM's founder, once called a young manager into his office. As this young man had apparently lost $10 million, he was expecting the worst: 'I guess you want my resignation.' Watson replied, 'You can't be serious. We spent $10 million educating you.'

To learn effectively from mistakes and to incorporate such an attitude in knowledge-based businesses, professionals' selected learning strategies need to include the ability to give structured feedback. This is something that can be taught and in fact does not take long. With practice in both giving and receiving constructive feedback, mistakes could become an invaluable forum for sharing new insights and removing blocks caused by fearful thinking.

> A consultancy company we know has put together a booklet called 'Our most famous mistakes' which is given to each new employee. Their Monday morning project meetings are guided by the question, 'What have you learned from your present assignments?

Competence Culture 7: Commitment to development through working via strategic partnerships and 'competence networks'

Since innovations often occur in interaction between people, a competence culture is characterized to a high degree by cooperating with people from a variety of professional backgrounds. Perhaps the most undervalued source of new knowledge is clients and 'competitors'. We believe that successful companies of the future will involve their clients in their competence development. In fact we go one step further and claim that the key to success lies in treating your clients as employees and your 'competitors' as developers.

> One highly successful international training company in London constantly creates new projects and partnerships with colleagues and 'competitors'. Its core skills lie in helping people become powerful communicators. As the organization is highly flexible and its mission is total commitment to practical results, the company can team up with virtually any kind of professional to achieve new business. Its range of projects is extensive and comprises medical, legal and management consultancy experts.

The word 'competitor' has negative connotations for many people, so we recommend looking on competitors as those people who have complementary knowledge to yours. Competitors can also be seen as potential strategic partners. As learning is a process, there is much to be gained from learning how to proceed with those who are striving to find what you want to find. In fact, to compete means 'to strive together'.

Involve your 'competitors', subcontractors, suppliers and/or business partners. Instead of fighting about 'market share', why not share your markets and through effective marketing make the *total* market grow? This type of strategy is typical of what has been called the 'virtual corporation'. Such a corporation is a temporary network of companies that come together quickly to exploit fast-changing opportunities. Companies in a 'virtual corporation' can share costs, skills and access to global markets—and contribute what they are best at.

To work together in 'strategic alliances', people really need to understand one another. To acquire knowledge by working through alliances, professionals need to understand their partner's strengths and weaknesses and how acquiring particular skills will benefit their competitiveness. Above all, such alliances have to be built on 'win–win' relationships.

Concerning internal 'competence networks', one practical model for mapping such relationships is outlined by David Krackhardt and Jeffrey Hanson. They refer to three networks based on advice, trust and communication. Advice networks comprise those people whom others depend on to solve problems and provide technical information. Trust networks refer to those people who share sensitive information with one another and support one another, and communication networks consist of those people who talk about work-related matters on a regular basis. The most critical factor of 'competence networks', according to Krackhardt and Hanson, is the time and care that is put into them so that when knowledge professionals need information or advice, their networks respond quickly.

Competence Culture 8: Clear concepts and methods for 'production' and quality assurance

One of the challenges of a knowledge organization is to capitalize on intellectual property, eg software, copyrights, patents, processes, information databases and expert systems, drawings and technologies. Through such means, organizational profitability can be created out of intangible assets. However, in most companies the management of intellectual capital is still uncharted territory and few executives know how to navigate it.

One of the companies entering this uncharted territory is **Skandia AFS**, a multinational financial services and insurance company. Skandia AFS has one of the world's first managers with the title 'director of intellectual capital'. Leif Edvinsson has held this post since it was created in 1991. He says, 'My mission is to convert

IQ to ECU. This is done through identifying, capturing, cultivating and capitalizing on Skandia's intellectual assets. I work with three interrelated corporate functions: human resources, business development and information technology systems to enhance productivity and speed up learning processes. One example is how we "capitalized" our experience in how to reduce the time factor in market penetration. We developed an information technology approach system, "The Prototype", which would help our new start-up offices and enable them to run their business within less than half of the usual time. The focus on intellectual capital, information technology and culture has proved itself to be a lever enabling us to keep a sustainable 30–40 per cent growth rate for a number of years.'

The time has come for the knowledge sector to industrialize production. Knowledge is adapted to the client's needs and there has been a conviction among professionals that 'how to tackle the problem' is specific for each individual client relationship and assignment.

But competent clients have the right to demand efficiency, and many professionals are paid on the basis of time spent. There is also a tendency to 'package' the offer, not in terms of selling methods but to supply a specific result at a fixed price. To be profitable this way, the knowledge company has to work with its productivity factors.

One issue that is frequently debated is, 'Are there any large-scale advantages in the knowledge sector?' From certain perspectives, the answer is yes. These perspectives are linked to developing knowledge, productivity *and* quality assurance.

Cap Gemini Sogeti, one of the world's leading transnational IT consultancies, based in France, says that thanks to its leadership position it can be involved in the IT industry's major R&D initiatives. It can thereby maintain a constant dialogue with major universities and research institutes.

To assure profitability, Cap Gemini Sogeti's managers have been assigned by the company's owners to develop an internal system and concept for quality assurance, efficiency and productivity. They say, 'If there is one thing we have learnt over the years, it's that no two projects are the same. Each customer, each undertaking is a special case and needs a personalized approach. But there are common elements.' These elements have been crystallized into a system called Perform.

Although this system is fundamentally a project quality plan, it also acts simultaneously as a means of providing each project with management, disciplines and tools. These tools ensure that at any time, managers know the exact status of all aspects of a project.

Perform also contains quality audits which act as an early warning system to enable managers to pinpoint and rectify any faults immediately. Perform is linked to ISO 9000 certification and is implemented internally through training, handbooks and computer systems. Perform assists each project leader and all team members to take a structured approach to international projects. Multinational teams can be put together in a minimum amount of time while still ensuring that the same quality standards are applied throughout the world.

LEARNING PROCESSES

The rest of this chapter focuses on disarmingly simple, highly practical approaches to internal development that tend to be overlooked. Since time is your major bottleneck, you need to start where you are right now. Therefore we will initiate the next step by asking: How does your company organize its learning processes so that they are integrated with day-to-day work and business development?

One way of enhancing your knowledge company's development on an everyday basis is to divide your learning into four interrelated processes:

1. Personal profiling of knowledge professionals.
2. 'RDM'—Research, development and marketing.
3. Development of experience in assignments and client projects.
4. Feedback and evaluation.

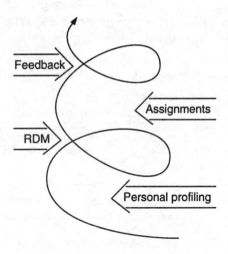

Figure 6.3 The interrelated processes of learning

Personal profiling of knowledge professionals

The ability to build on and enhance interactive learning is based on how attracted team members, colleagues and managers are to one another's knowledge and to one another as people.

Therefore, effective interactive learning highlights professionals' skills in communicating with people from diverse backgrounds. Here you need to have a clear picture of your knowledge potential and how you can continually develop it and 'market' it. To do this you need a regular and consistent sequence of feedback from your environment which means you have to get to know your colleagues well.

We focus first on knowledge professionals' responsibility to 'market' themselves internally to *clarify* their knowledge and value to those with whom they are to work. This is a way for the entire organization to learn and to understand the complete range of competences that exist in a knowledge company. The total sum is obtained through adding up each individual's knowledge profile.

An expert model

Robert Kelley and Janet Caplan outline what they call an expert model for engineers, which comprises nine work strategies. Four of these are: 'Taking initiative: accepting responsibility above and beyond your stated job, volunteering for additional activities, and promoting new ideas. Self-management: regulating your own work commitments, time, performance level, and career growth. Networking: getting direct and immediate access to coworkers with technical expertise and sharing your own knowledge with those who need it. Show-and-tell: presenting your ideas persuasively in writing or oral form.'

Taking initiative was identified as the core strategy of the expert model and one of the people interviewed suggested making a 'checklist for taking initiative'. This list gives a sample of specific actions and behaviours that characterize the strategy. For example, 'I think about and try to document how my idea would save the company money or bring in new business.' Another example includes, 'I construct a plan for selling my idea to people in the company.'

To be able to communicate and cooperate well with other people, you need good rapport and good interpersonal 'chemistry'. Ian McDermott, Director of International Teaching Seminars, says, 'Rapport can be described as a cooperative mode of communication between one or more persons and is, quite simply, the basis of all successful communication. It is the oil that lubricates every relationship . . . Professionals in any field who don't know how to build and maintain it pay dearly through lost credibility and lost contracts, lost promotion and lost pay. However, to get on with others, there is a very interesting thing that is necessary—you first need to get on with yourself.'

In addition to rapport, it is useful to see cooperation with colleagues and networks in knowledge-based businesses as an exchange process. Getting to grips with this exchange process is a key to influencing behaviour and providing someone with what they need. Something that others need can be called currency, which is a useful metaphor for 'lubricating' knowledge-based relationships.

Newcomers to knowledge companies could be assigned mentors and then, after they have been in the company for a while, they could choose their own. Ideally, everyone should have a mentor.

> One company we know of does not give extra pay for being a mentor but such responsibility can pay off, since 75 per cent of the company's owners rank one another during the course of every year. In other words, the more a professional is viewed by his or her colleagues as having contributed to their competence, the more that professional's salary is raised during the forthcoming year!

Empowering everyone in a knowledge company through joint ownership, for example, means that everyone is responsible for their own goals and budgets and learning how to reach them. As a result, many consultants in knowledge companies are beginning to receive professional guidance in their role towards their clients. They are also acquiring help in how to behave towards their colleagues.

'RDM'—Research, development and marketing

It is the time you invest in internal development and marketing that pays off at a later date. What is important is how you optimize this time so that you obtain maximum returns. Three approaches to RDM learning are outlined below.

Combine knowledge goals with marketing goals

For example, you could:

- take part in a market and client research project—be responsible for scanning a certain area of a market;
- write and publish papers, articles and books—this forces you to think through the subject from different perspectives;
- arrange seminars with external parties, eg clients, 'competitors', researchers, clients' business associations, and learn from them, be a teacher on a course, make a presentation at a client's conference, meeting, etc or an internal meeting;

- sponsor a research project;
- award a prize and be one of the judges;
- take on positions of responsibility in your own or your clients' professional associations and learn from the interaction with them.

Dr George Simons, principal of **George Simons International** based in Santa Cruz, USA, produces publications and training programmes together with colleagues in the USA and Europe for the multicultural business environment. He specializes in diversity issues and defines diversity as: the universe of cultural resources (values, habits, skills, knowledge, customs, learnings, etc) which exists in a mixed group of people because of their variety. Diversity is the aggregate creative and productive potential of such a group.

Through producing leading-edge training games in the field of diversity, George and his colleagues are forced constantly to study the international business environment and current media to keep their consultancy services, games and training of trainers up to date. While leading seminars throughout the world, George constantly stresses the value of sharing knowledge and its importance in developing everyone's understanding—including his own. Through sharing insights and learnings with clients and colleagues, George gains constant competence from his assignments. It all adds up to making him an even better 'cabinet maker or weaver'.

Another important source of research, development and marketing is writing books. To help colleagues, leaders and professionals build on their understanding of multicultural teams and projects, George has co-authored a recently published book called *Transcultural leadership*. True to his learning approach, this book opens with the statement, 'We are all immigrants to the twenty-first century'.

Combine knowledge goals with the development of quality and methods

For example:

- take part in internal development of methods;
- cooperate with researchers in your own fields and those of your clients;
- participate in internal quality development programmes;
- arrange a 'competence network' of colleagues and 'competitors' to create ideas on how to solve certain problems;
- be responsible for scanning a certain area of expertise, for example research, and transfer it to the rest of the organization.

In terms of how you could participate in internal development programmes, we refer once again to the research carried out by Robert Kelley and Janet Caplan. In 1990, 40 engineers at Bell Labs and 25 engineers at another high-tech telecommunications company were asked to evaluate themselves. The engineers were to answer the following four questions every day for two weeks:

- How productive were you today?
- How did you measure your productivity?
- What caused you to be either productive or unproductive today?
- Did you get feedback about your productivity?

What emerged from the survey was that practically none of the engineers had any clear idea of what activities added value to their company. In fact, there was only one engineer who one day measured his productivity as 'amount of my work making a direct contribution to the company.'

Combine knowledge development goals with personal goals

For example, you want to see another country. Why not find a person in that country to network with? In this way you could develop new market possibilities and personal experiences.

One of our Italian colleagues is the epitome of an entrepreneurial person who is in line with what she wants, and with what also benefits her company and family. She runs a successful auditing company situated in northern Italy. She loves England and learning and so do her two children. What our colleague did was to contact a local language training company and through them obtained the name of a school in England where she and her children studied English one summer. That was a few years ago and since then her international contact network has rapidly expanded into new business areas and ways of helping her children to become multilingual.

* * *

Pavla Kruzela, another colleague of ours, had a very long-term personal goal—to learn to play golf. Pavla is Czech and works internationally as a management consultant. This is what she told us when she described how she combined a personal goal with a knowledge goal:

'I started thinking about golf ten years ago. However, it wasn't until some time later whilst carrying out research in companies in India that I first started playing. It took a little while until I really became a fan of golf. I suddenly realized how I could combine the joy of learning to play golf well with the pleasure of doing business and carrying out interviews whilst walking round the golf course.

'Although I practice other sports such as tennis, swimming and jogging, in my opinion, golf is the most demanding and challenging sport. One plays against the ball and one's skill lies in technique and concentration rather than sheer physical strength. Although a trainer can help you improve your technique, it is up to you yourself to improve your mental skills. The handicap system, in particular, contributes towards golfers constantly having a new goal to aim for and there is a delight in learning how to be successful in both long-distance shots and in the immediacy of the putting green.'

Development of experience in assignments and client projects

Your competitiveness lies in how you use the time your clients pay for. Professionals increasingly need organizations in order to leverage the experiences they make in a more turbulent business world. In this respect they are not quite like the autonomous, independent professionals of the past.

Professionals need to learn how to work in teams since in this way they can gain help in building on their past and current experiences. They can also get help in preparing for new experiences and hints on how to document and communicate what they have learned—both to themselves and to others.

Examples of ways of learning while carrying out assignments are:

- taking on the challenging, front-line assignments (challenge zone);
- having two colleagues on one assignment with the purpose of learning from two different approaches and reflecting together on their outcomes;
- the knowledge company could 'sponsor' a client assignment that is valuable as a source of new knowledge;
- use your client as a resource, eg in developing methods. By giving your knowledge in education, for example, the client can systemize and document the method (developing a method in partnership).

Two language and communication training consultants in a high-tech organization often teach as a team at specific intervals. Through this process they are able to mirror one another's competences. They benefit by seeing not only what the other trainer does but also gaining greater clarification of their own methods. Together they are able to put into words the nature of the powerful processes they 'plant' in their training programmes to enable their clients to reach their goals.

The results of these insights in terms of development are numerous. Clients, co-trainers and colleagues become further inspired to gain additional insights into their own thinking processes. They see the power of language and how it affects their behaviour. They gain access to a never-ending spiral.

The attitude during this phase is to learn from your assignment. Another possible resource is to have a quality controller who checks with the client during a large assignment and then gives feedback to the team.

Learning through feedback and evaluation

Identify success factors and risks through systematic feedback. Knowledge professionals can acquire valuable feedback from:

- clients;
- team members;
- managers;
- themselves;
- the network—external partners, eg journalists.

At **Design for Business** feedback and evaluation are organized on a day-to-day basis, mainly through reviews of daily planning and target setting and a weekly subjective evaluation of performance using a simple scale of 1–10 which is used to develop a profile showing variations. Comments are added to elaborate on significant points.

Examples of situations to create:

- Arrange a follow-up meeting with your client. Invite some of your colleagues to join this meeting. For example, an advertising agency invited young, junior consultants to clients' follow-up meetings.
- Let a researcher or student make an evaluation based on interviews with clients and communicate the results to your whole group.
- Follow up an assignment of one of your team members or colleagues by interviewing the clients concerned.
- Arrange an internal 'audit' and go through what each professional has achieved for the clients and has learned for the future.
- Set goals for yourself on an annual basis and follow your progress through in a 'personal balance sheet'.

Anna Kahn of A-Quality, an independent consultant specializing in quality issues for knowledge-based companies, has developed a self/group assessment tool called the 'Personal Balance Sheet' (PBS). One of the steps in the PBS consists of each professional answering a checklist. For example, knowledge professionals review the year according to such factors as their:

- total revenue for the past year in relation to the budget;
- percentage of 'renewed' business;
- involvement in projects together with colleagues in the company;
- development of competence networks;
- current client structure compared to desired client structure.

After completing this checklist, the knowledge professional then discusses his or her PBS together with three or four other consultants. Anna stresses the importance of carrying out this discussion in a relaxed environment where the participants know one another well. This dialogue is followed up every six months and knowledge leaders can use the information to monitor the development of success factors for the company.

Together with Anna Kahn, we have developed our own version of the Personal Balance Sheet. This has been designed to match the specific business requirements of knowledge professionals and their organizations.

PERSONAL BALANCE SHEET			
Complete the balance sheet by inserting the appropriate number of points against each statement.			
	Yes, very well (4)	Yes, quite well (3)	No, not so well (2)	No, not at all (1)
Choice of client			
I have a good picture of my own client structure.	☐	☐	☐	☐
I have a good picture of my own assignment structure.	☐	☐	☐	☐
My client and assignment structures have developed in accordance with the company's/ department's choice of clients and assignments.	☐	☐	☐	☐
The number of new and 'old' clients correspond with the objectives set up for this period.	☐	☐	☐	☐
Client information			
I have developed routines for finding out developments and trends on the markets of our chosen client target categories.	☐	☐	☐	☐
I have regularly found out how clients' needs develop.	☐	☐	☐	☐

	Yes, very well (4)	Yes, quite well (3)	No, not so well (2)	No, not at all (1)
Chain of client value				
I have, together with clients, established goals for every assignment.	☐	☐	☐	☐
I have, together with clients, evaluated my assignments at certain intervals according to a specific system.	☐	☐	☐	☐
I have reached those process goals of change that were expected by clients as well as creating additional value.	☐	☐	☐	☐
I have received new assignments from previous clients (sign of their satisfaction).	☐	☐	☐	☐
I have been recommended by long-standing clients and key people in the contact network.	☐	☐	☐	☐
Contact network				
I have initiated and developed strategic contacts that are aligned to our client choice.	☐	☐	☐	☐
I have initiated and developed strategic contacts for my/our competence development.	☐	☐	☐	☐
I have worked with external and internal key people to increase credibility and competence.	☐	☐	☐	☐
Client education				
I have clarified how we view future developments within our chosen client categories' business areas, the threats and possibilities we see for them. I have, for example, activated important issues, given good advice, explained links we see, etc.	☐	☐	☐	☐

	Yes, very well (4)	Yes, quite well (3)	No, not so well (2)	No, not at all (1)
I have supplied 'old' and long-standing clients with new knowledge to strengthen their roles as recommenders (and thus sell new knowledge).	☐	☐	☐	☐
I have, through client education, contributed towards creating a spontaneous demand for our knowledge.	☐	☐	☐	☐

Channels of communication

I have broadcast our ideas (shared knowledge) through, for example, publishing, giving presentations, writing articles and reports, etc.	☐	☐	☐	☐
I have satisfactorily kept my clients informed during the process of the assignment.	☐	☐	☐	☐
I have kept in contact with previous clients.	☐	☐	☐	☐

Competence development

I have taken on a sufficient number of challenging assignments.	☐	☐	☐	☐
I have, through cooperation via internal and external networks, increased my competence in accordance with my knowledge goals.	☐	☐	☐	☐
I have actively contributed towards my colleagues' development by sharing my knowledge generously.	☐	☐	☐	☐
Total points in each column:	_____	_____	_____	_____

Total: _____

Summary

Competence development stresses the importance of a learning culture and represents the culture and cornerstones of a competent learning environment. To conclude, we recommend that you ask yourself the following questions and that you commit yourself by writing your answers in the space provided. The actual process of writing gives you an opportunity both to formulate an idea/thought and then to review it from a different perspective. Writing down your thoughts provides a way of having a learning dialogue with yourself.

ASK YOURSELF AND YOUR TEAM MEMBERS:

- Has your team ever celebrated a mistake? What would happen if it did?
- Think about your chosen client categories. What is happening in each target market? What knowledge will they need from you in three years from now? (your knowledge goals)
- What would you look for as indices of increased productivity in, for example, your own learning processes and that of your team?

References

Becker, Frank (1992) 'The Eternal Coffee Break', *The Economist*, March.

Geary, James (1993) 'Original synergy', *Holland Herald*, October.

Katzenbach, Jon R and Douglas K Smith (1993) *The Wisdom of Teams: creating the High Performance Organization*, Harvard Business School Press, Boston.

Kelley, Robert and Janet Caplan (1993) 'How Bell Labs Create Star Performers', *Harvard Business Review*, July–August.

Krackhardt, David and Jeffrey R Hanson (1993) 'Informal Networks: The Company', *Harvard Business Review*, July–August.

McDermott, Ian (1993) 'Managing people: how rapport and congruence can increase your influence', *ITS Journal*, 3, June.

Olofsson, Peter (1993) 'Vi måste skapa korsdrag', *Inforama,* 2, Västerås, Sweden.

Peters, Thomas J (1992) *Liberation Management*, Alfred A Knopf, New York.

Simons, George F, Carmen Vazquez and Philip R Harris (1993) *Transcultural Leadership: Empowering the Diverse Workforce*, Gulf Publishing Company, Houston, Texas.

7

The Role of the Marketing Developer

'This places me in the position of "consultant to the consultants".'

Gunilla Ramell

This chapter deals with the role of the full-time marketing professional in the knowledge organization.

Sell Your Knowledge is built on the conviction that knowledge professionals themselves have the responsibility to create, develop and retain client relationships. To enable and help them to manage their role as 'part-time marketers', some organizations have created an internal support function, a marketing or information unit. Since auditors, solicitors, consultants, etc are still relatively new to marketing, most marketing positions are in larger firms. In this chapter we present the main aspects of this person's role, whom we call the marketing developer.

EXPECTATIONS FROM THE ORGANIZATION

What are the organization's expectations of the marketing developer? In our opinion, they range from leadership in business development and marketing to support and coordination of activities.

Tim Kasso, director of marketing at solicitors Nabarro Nathanson put the question 'What do you want from marketing?' to representatives of five professional fields (accountants, engineers, solicitors, surveyors and architects). The answers give the following view of expectations from partners and professionals. They want their marketer to:

- encourage, stimulate and advise the professional partners in making themselves into effective marketers;
- set and clarify commercial (not just financial) goals;
- bring together diverse skills and interests to a common understanding of focused activities;
- facilitate change;
- identify new markets/client categories;
- develop the client database.

A SYNTHESIS OF DIFFERENT SKILLS

The functions of the marketing developer of a knowledge company are not yet fully established. However, to facilitate discussion, we have outlined four major roles that require different background competences and aim at different results (see Figure 7.1). In small firms the four roles have to be managed and integrated by one person, whereas in larger firms the roles can be assigned to different people.

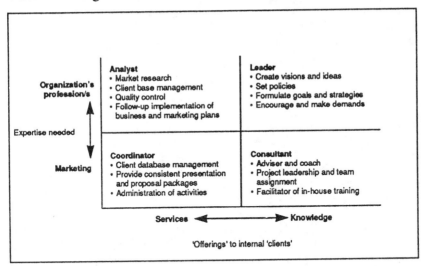

Figure 7.1   Roles of the marketing developer

THE ROLE IN PRACTICE

How can these roles be carried out in practice? This depends on the company's needs and the background of the marketing developer. Gunilla Ramell, director of client information services at John R McKean & Co, describes her view of her role as follows:

Reporting to the senior partner in charge of marketing, I view my role as one of facilitator and coordinator of the company's business development function. This places me in the position of 'consultant to the (CPA) consultants' themselves who, by necessity, maintain responsibility for creating, developing and maintaining client relations for our firm. While my role is to stimulate, motivate and coordinate our marketing efforts, the CPAs act as the company's sales force. The purpose of my job is to:

- Ensure that existing client relationships are satisfactorily maintained.
- Expand the firm's market share in practice areas which we currently serve (eg providing cost and profitability consulting services to law firms and other closely held businesses).
- Develop new potentially profitable market niches, for example, by extending cost and profitability consulting services to also include physicians and other professionals.

As the company's full-time marketing professional, the roles I perform in order to achieve those objectives include the following:

- Enhance potential client awareness of John R McKean & Co and its services through vehicles such as publicity and a limited amount of advertising.
- Accelerate the process of generating new, 'qualified' leads, primarily by means of direct mail and seminars for prospective clients.
- Educate the market through general seminars and other less formal group discussions.
- Encourage marketing contacts by all members of the firm, including acting as a catalyst for such contacts and coaching members prior to telephone or in-person presentations.
- Develop strong presentation and proposal packages for potential client engage ments, including keeping an eye on the quality and consistency of our external marketing communications.
- Communicate with current clients on matters of ongoing significance.
- Suggest strategies to enhance client retention.
- Conduct market research by gathering information on prospective clients.
- Gather competitive intelligence by analysing competitors' strengths and weaknesses.

The ability to provide both knowledge *and* services is not always easy to combine in one person. The knowledge part of the role demands proactive behaviour (long-term thinking and taking initiatives), self-esteem, ability to create trust and competence in teaching. It means spending time in the worlds of the internal 'clients' rather than in a separate office. The service part of the role requires responsiveness (acting at short notice), reliability and accuracy.

SELECTING A MARKETING DEVELOPER

What personality traits are necessary for a person working full time with marketing in a knowledge company, which is often 'closely held' or partner owned?

Richard Chaplin is the initiator and managing director of the Professional Services Marketing Group, based in London, an international network for individuals involved in the provision of marketing services within professional service firms. He is also managing director of Professional Marketing International, a search consultancy firm specializing in searching for marketing professionals for positions in consultancies and other professional firms.

Chaplin points out that selecting and retaining the right marketers continues to cause difficulties for professional firms. The main reasons are that most professional firms are still relatively new to marketing. Also personnel departments in professional firms are generally not familiar with hiring marketers. 'Until recently,' he says, 'in the eyes of most marketers, the sector of professional services was a backwater. Many of those marketers currently employed will find it difficult to compete with the new breed of marketers now entering the sector. Such individuals, with a personality capable of adapting quickly to a partnership culture, are attracted by an expanding sector, higher-than-average salaries and a new set of marketing challenges.'

Professional Marketing International published research carried out by Strategic Marketing Connections into the desired personality profile of a marketer in a professional service firm (Professional Marketing International, 1993). The results can act as a guide when selecting a marketer for a knowledge organization. Important conclusions from the research are:

- Leadership skills are key skills at all levels since important decisions are often expected about the firm's marketing activities.
- Successful marketers working in professional firms need to be more sensitive to the political currents than their counterparts in other sectors. They tend to thrive in a role that is more tactical than strategic, take a 'back seat' in discussions rather than provide ideas.
- Implementation should not be ignored. Marketers who concentrate only on strategy at the expense of day-to-day activities are embarking on a dangerous path.

An ideal marketer is not overly concerned with job titles. A good marketer will prove his or her worth by gaining the respect of the partners, and will then influence those partners to alter their patterns of behaviour and become more client focused. Promotion will then be a natural consequence.

Richard Chaplin paints the following portrait of a typical marketer working in a professional firm: 'The ideal candidate for a marketing position has some previous experience in marketing professional services. Marketing qualifications are not seen as essential, although a university degree is expected. The marketing professional should be a dynamic individual with a lot of drive. S/he is an *organizer*, hard-working, with common sense and self-discipline, a natural *leader* who is able to treat all contributors to a group on the basis of their merits, a *coordinator* who, through tactical rather than strategic means, coordinates others rather than being seen as the provider of ideas. S/he is very sensitive to people and their vibrations in devising and implementing marketing plans and activities.'

THE INTERNAL COMPETENCE CENTRE

One way of looking at—and developing—the marketing developer's position as an 'internal consultancy' is to view it as an internal competence centre and support function. If you 'live as you learn' you define the business idea of your unit/function and communicate it to your 'market' in order to create a demand for your knowledge and services. To do this you can use the seven Cs. The first four Cs provide you with a means for formulating your business idea:

- *Choice of clients*. Define your internal clients, eg partners and managers.
- *Client information*. Identify their needs for your knowledge and services. What do managers/partners need to be able to fulfil their role as business developers and enable professionals to fulfil theirs as marketers?
- *Chain of client values*. What value do you intend to create for your internal clients and the organization? Are you going to act mainly as a competence centre, providing knowledge and advice, or as a service centre, carrying out tasks for them? Or a combination?
- *Competence*. Which are your competitive advantages (the knowledge and services could be bought externally or carried out by some of the internal clients themselves).

Having answered these questions you have carried out the analysis and created your own desired image. The next part of your internal marketing process is to communicate your knowledge in order to create the *right* demand, the demand you want. If you want to act as a knowledge provider, you have to take the initiative yourself since people cannot ask for knowledge which they do not know exists. Use the fifth and sixth Cs:

■ *Contact network.* Internal key people for you to cooperate with can be people in the HRD department, the information department, the editor of the internal newsletter. Externally you should communicate with your own professional network and its journal/newsletter, key people at the professional association of your 'clients', editors at their professional journal (to get information), etc.

■ *Customer education and communication channels.* If you want to enhance the level of activity and create an interest in learning and practising marketing and relationship management you could invite a marketing researcher or an external consultant to give a presentation or a seminar; invite a partner or a marketing professional from a company operating in quite a different professional field to share experiences and ideas with your partners, perhaps initiating a 'benchmarking' process with them; publish ideas in the internal 'newsletter'; review new books and trends in relationship marketing.

You could also arrange client audits; initiate internal development programmes to encourage marketing activities and efforts; initiate a reward for good marketing and client development.

Do not forget the seventh C:

■ *Competence development.* Your own learning is crucial. Follow research, initiate research, study marketing efforts in other professional fields. Meet colleagues nationally and internationally. Contribute to your development through publishing articles and papers (this will also enhance your internal image). Develop educational programmes. Last, and not least, follow up your activities and let your internal 'clients' evaluate your contributions.

IN-HOUSE TRAINING AND DEVELOPMENT

A problem facing many knowledge organizations is that many professionals refrain from taking responsibility for marketing and client relationship management. Why? What are the hindrances to conducting goal-oriented and efficient marketing in the professional firm? David

Maister has captured this as follows: 'for many professional firms, the "marketing problem" is frequently not really about marketing. Rather, it is a managerial problem: how to ensure that "things happen".'

One way to get to grips with participation is to initiate an in-house training programme. The goals for such a programme can be formulated in different dimensions. Whether you design and carry out the programme yourself, or hire a consultant, be sure to define the purposes of the time invested. The list below can act as a source of inspiration when discussing intentions, goals and possible evaluation measurements.

After the programme the participants are supposed to have obtained new knowledge, new attitudes and abilities (short term), carried out activities and achieved results (long term). The various levels of goals can be defined as follows:

Knowledge and attitudes at an individual level

■ Consciousness of their own role as 'part-time marketers'.
■ Knowledge of theory and methods for marketing of knowledge and services.
■ Motivation to act in their role as marketers.
■ A sense of professional pride and self-esteem in their role.
■ Potential to act in order to create and retain client relationships.

Knowledge and attitudes at a group level

■ A common 'language' and methodology for marketing.
■ An 'eagle view' of and understanding of the company/unit and its development.
■ Better insight into others' expertise as a basis for 'cross-selling'.
■ Enhanced business orientation.
■ A joint vision and commitment to the company's vision and goals.
■ Team spirit and ability to cooperate.

Activities and related effects

As part of the programme you can have participants carry out action plans and marketing activities. From this your organization will obtain:

■ more actions taken in marketing;
■ more feedback/follow-up actions;
■ more contented clients (can be measured by feedback and client acknowledgements);

- more goal-oriented marketing (to do the right things is more important than to do things right);
- more time-efficient marketing activities;
- greater spontaneous demand from new and old clients;
- more contented clients and a stronger reputation;
- faster learning processes.

Financial results

- Enhanced profitability.
- Enhanced return on investment in marketing.

Design the programme as an action-learning process. The facilitator acts as a leader, teacher, guide and coach. Think through which sections you can lead yourself and in which sections you need to involve others, eg external consultants, internal senior partners and clients. Plan the learning process so that it is integrated with annual business and market planning.

Spread training sessions/meetings over a period of about three to six months. In between you act as supporter and coach, while the teams do their planning and activities. At the end of the process the participants should have formulated plans, including a division of responsibilities and time budgets and schedules. If the programme involves partners/managers it aims at a jointly produced business and quality development plan. If it involves team members you aim at market activity plans for each team connected to specific target markets.

Have participants work in small self-selected teams, either those working in the same area of expertise or those working with a specific client category. Let each team appoint a team leader. A group of 20 participants, for example, can be divided into four small teams. Allow the process to be an opportunity for trial and error. To stimulate learning and cooperation, avoid competition between the participants. Instead, create an atmosphere of openness and generosity, where learning from each other's mistakes is considered as important as learning from success stories.

Explain to the participants that this is not a traditional course where they can take a back-seat role. They are involved in a continuous, interactive workshop. Explain to the managers of the participants that they are co-responsible for the results and therefore need to attend and support the facilitator in the discussions. If there is, or recently has been, turbulence in the organization, this will show in terms of a 'backlash'. However, this is not to be considered as a hindrance or threat to the action-learning process, as long as the managers deal with the situation.

View and design the training programme as developing a methodology for leading and conducting the business and market planning process.

After the programme, give managers regular support so they can continue to act as leaders of the planning process by involving their teams. Point out that they cannot expect short-term profitability results. Business development and marketing of knowledge is a long-term investment that has to be allotted what it needs to produce returns—competence and time.

A CHALLENGING FIELD

As described in Chapter 1, the entire arena of knowledge professionals is continually being reconceptualized. As a result, the marketing developer has an increasing responsibility to help knowledge professionals to translate these reconceptualizations directly into *action*.

In the new economy, where intangibles such as knowledge and services are emerging markets, marketers therefore have huge unexplored regions to enter. We emphasize the need for research in the field of marketing knowledge. Interdisciplinary approaches will have to be initiated, eg between human resource developers, information technology experts and marketing developers.

The marketing of knowledge is *the* challenge for global business.

References

Kasso, Tim (1993) 'What do you want from marketing?', *Professional Marketing*, Vol 1, Issue 2, April.

Maister, David H (1993) *Professional Service Firm Management*, Maister Associates, Boston.

Professional Marketing International (1993) *Personality profile of marketers*, A survey based on 100 'Belbin' psychometric tests carried out by Strategic Marketing Connections, June, London.

Strategic Marketing Connections (1991) *Marketing attitudes in accountants, solicitors and other professional services firms*, executive summary of a study of the perceptions of in-house marketing professionals, Strategic Marketing Connections, London.

Index

158 *Sell Your Knowledge*